# A Stillness

## in the STORM

## ANABEL GILLHAM

**HARVEST HOUSE PUBLISHERS**
Eugene, Oregon 97402

**A STILLNESS IN THE STORM**

Copyright © 1995 by Anabel Gillham
Published by Harvest House Publishers
Eugene, Oregon 97402

Gillham, Anabel.
    A stillness in the storm / Anabel Gillham.
        p.   cm.
    ISBN 1-56507-287-1
    1. Christian life.   2. Meditations.   I. Title.
BV4501.2.G51116    1995
242—dc20                                            94-47487
                                                        CIP

95 96 97 98 99 00 01 02 03 / 9 8 7 6 5 4 3 2 1

*If I should write a book or two*
*That helped a lot—or helped a few*
*That book would be—like my life—like me*
<u>*Dedicated to You.*</u>

*To You—Lord.*

*The thoughts that are written I merely*
*transcribed for You. It's been hard to*
*share some of them—they're so intensely*
*personal—but that wasn't my choice to*
*make.*

*So here they are. Please use them, Lord, to*
*bless others who are—as I was so many*
*times—hurting, confused, misunderstood,*
*lonely—just needing someone to say, "I*
*understand."*

# Contents

1. The Song of My Heart . . . . . . . . . . . . . . . . . . . . . 3

2. Confirm Your Presence, Lord . . . . . . . . . . . . . . . 4

3. An Intimate Moment . . . . . . . . . . . . . . . . . . . . . 6

4. Loving Reminders . . . . . . . . . . . . . . . . . . . . . . 9

5. The Dwelling Place of God . . . . . . . . . . . . . . . 11

6. From Trash to Treasure . . . . . . . . . . . . . . . . . 20

7. The Keeper of the Keys . . . . . . . . . . . . . . . . . 23

8. Just Because You're Mine . . . . . . . . . . . . . . . . 25

9. A Childlike Heart . . . . . . . . . . . . . . . . . . . . . . 30

10. Close to the Father . . . . . . . . . . . . . . . . . . . . . 33

11. Our Time Together . . . . . . . . . . . . . . . . . . . . . 36

12. Undoing the Deceiver . . . . . . . . . . . . . . . . . . . 38

13. Nothing Can Separate Us . . . . . . . . . . . . . . . . 44

14. A New Definition of New . . . . . . . . . . . . . . . . 46

15. His Love for Me . . . . . . . . . . . . . . . . . . . . . . . 49

16. The Master's Voice . . . . . . . . . . . . . . . . . . . . . 51

17. Teach Me, Lord . . . . . . . . . . . . . . . . . . . . . . . 56

18. Sweet and Sour Chicken . . . . . . . . . . . . . . . . . 59

19. What Is God Saying to You? . . . . . . . . . . . . . . 62

20. The Bedrock . . . . . . . . . . . . . . . . . . . . . . . . . 66

21. Seeing Jesus . . . . . . . . . . . . . . . . . . . . . . . . . 69

22. Please Love Me. . . . . . . . . . . . . . . . . . . . . . . . 72

23. Simple, But Maybe Not Easy . . . . . . . . . . . . . 74

24. Under His Wings . . . . . . . . . . . . . . . . . . . . . 76

25. Lions, Bears, and Giants . . . . . . . . . . . . . . . 78

26. A Message for the Master . . . . . . . . . . . . . . 81

27. Knowing Where the Rabbits Are. . . . . . . . . . . 83

28. Love That Never Lets You Go. . . . . . . . . . . . . 86

29. Casting Your Burdens on Him . . . . . . . . . . . . 89

30. Trusting Him with My Burdens. . . . . . . . . . . . 93

31. A Very Present Help. . . . . . . . . . . . . . . . . . . 95

32. A Worm with Wings . . . . . . . . . . . . . . . . . . . 97

33. Refreshment in the Desert . . . . . . . . . . . . . . 99

34. A Friend of Jesus . . . . . . . . . . . . . . . . . . . . 104

35. Free to Serve . . . . . . . . . . . . . . . . . . . . . . . 108

36. Doing God's Will. . . . . . . . . . . . . . . . . . . . . 111

37. Going Home. . . . . . . . . . . . . . . . . . . . . . . . 113

38. New Beginnings . . . . . . . . . . . . . . . . . . . . . 117

39. Everyday Miracles . . . . . . . . . . . . . . . . . . . 120

40. Promised Suffering, Promised Comfort. . . . . . 122

41. Grace, Not Deliverance . . . . . . . . . . . . . . . . 124

42. The Witness of Suffering . . . . . . . . . . . . . . . 126

43. From Fear to Trust. . . . . . . . . . . . . . . . . . . . 130

44. Sometimes I Wonder . . . . . . . . . . . . . . . . . . 134

45. The True Battle . . . . . . . . . . . . . . . . . . . . . . 137

46. Set Free by God's Truth . . . . . . . . . . . . . . . . . 139

47. Follow Me. . . . . . . . . . . . . . . . . . . . . . . . . . . . 143

48. Standing Strong in the Face of Death . . . . . . . 145

49. Evidence of God's Love . . . . . . . . . . . . . . . . . 147

50. A Stubborn Little Lamb . . . . . . . . . . . . . . . . . 149

51. The Whole Weight of Your Anxieties . . . . . . . 152

52. Does It Really Work? . . . . . . . . . . . . . . . . . . . 155

53. My Anxiety, God's Consolation. . . . . . . . . . . . 157

54. He Dwelt Among Us . . . . . . . . . . . . . . . . . . . . 159

55. An Eagle's Flight. . . . . . . . . . . . . . . . . . . . . . . 161

56. New—and Confident—in Christ. . . . . . . . . . . 166

57. Who Is Your Strength? . . . . . . . . . . . . . . . . . . 169

58. Daisies Don't Lie . . . . . . . . . . . . . . . . . . . . . . 173

59. An Instrument of God's Peace . . . . . . . . . . . . . 175

60. The Walk of Faith. . . . . . . . . . . . . . . . . . . . . . 179

61. Guard and Fight. . . . . . . . . . . . . . . . . . . . . . . 181

62. The Other Side of the Fence . . . . . . . . . . . . . . 184

63. When God Says No. . . . . . . . . . . . . . . . . . . . . 186

64. The Perfect Peace of God. . . . . . . . . . . . . . . . . 190

65. A Lot Like Peter. . . . . . . . . . . . . . . . . . . . . . . 192

66. A Letter from One Who Loves You. . . . . . . . . 195

67. Grace and Peace to You . . . . . . . . . . . . . . . . . 202

68. God's Perfect Timing . . . . . . . . . . . . . . . . . . . 204

69. Our Children, God's Children . . . . . . . . . . . . . 207

70. A God Who Hears. . . . . . . . . . . . . . . . . . . . . . 211

71. When Anger Overwhelms. . . . . . . . . . . . . . . 213

72. When the Storm Rages. . . . . . . . . . . . . . . . 217

73. The Father's Discipline. . . . . . . . . . . . . . . 219

74. A Troubled Soul . . . . . . . . . . . . . . . . . . . . . 222

75. Used by God in Hard Times . . . . . . . . . . . . 225

76. Sowing in Tears . . . . . . . . . . . . . . . . . . . . . 227

77. Fixing Our Eyes on Jesus. . . . . . . . . . . . . . 229

78. First Encounter . . . . . . . . . . . . . . . . . . . . . 231

79. Blazing a Path . . . . . . . . . . . . . . . . . . . . . . 233

80. When Jesus Was Gone . . . . . . . . . . . . . . . . 235

81. Finding Joy and Peace . . . . . . . . . . . . . . . . 237

82. Finding God in the Storm . . . . . . . . . . . . . 239

83. His Self-Portrait . . . . . . . . . . . . . . . . . . . . 241

84. The Sufferings of This World . . . . . . . . . . . 243

85. A Planned Pregnancy. . . . . . . . . . . . . . . . . 246

86. A Father's Words . . . . . . . . . . . . . . . . . . . . 248

87. A Song in the Night . . . . . . . . . . . . . . . . . . 251

88. Resting in God's Promises . . . . . . . . . . . . . 253

89. Safe at Last . . . . . . . . . . . . . . . . . . . . . . . . 256

90. God's Plan or Mine? . . . . . . . . . . . . . . . . . . 258

91. The Lamp and the Power. . . . . . . . . . . . . . . 260

92. The One to Turn To . . . . . . . . . . . . . . . . . . 263

93. If . . . . . . . . . . . . . . . . . . . . . . . . . . . . . . . . 265

94. The Test Drive . . . . . . . . . . . . . . . . . . . . . . 267

95. The Strength to Go On. . . . . . . . . . . . . . . . 269

96. Choosing Freedom . . . . . . . . . . . . . . . . . . . 271

97. Are You Settled in Your Mind? . . . . . . . . . . 274

98. Easter Thoughts for Every Day. . . . . . . . . . 277

99. Praying for Victory . . . . . . . . . . . . . . . . . . . 279

100. The Gift Too Wonderful for Words . . . . . . . . 281

101. Cleanse Me, Lord . . . . . . . . . . . . . . . . . . . . 283

102. Grace in Times of Need . . . . . . . . . . . . . . . 285

103. Thorns . . . . . . . . . . . . . . . . . . . . . . . . . . . . 287

104. No More Time to Pray. . . . . . . . . . . . . . . . . 289

105. Like a Child at Rest . . . . . . . . . . . . . . . . . . 291

106. My Stability . . . . . . . . . . . . . . . . . . . . . . . . 293

107. God's Plan for My Pain . . . . . . . . . . . . . . . . 295

108. Jesus' Transforming Touch . . . . . . . . . . . . . . 298

# Good morning!
## It's so nice to be with you. . . .

There are those times when we so want someone who cares, someone who will listen; someone to say, "I'm sorry you're hurting," to give godly counsel, to encourage us, to help us, perhaps, through a difficult time . . . to just sit down with us for a little while.

I would like to be this "someone" for you, to share my thoughts with you. Examine each thought carefully as you read to see if it is Truth. If it is, then grab it as you would a life preserver in a raging sea. (Is your sea raging just now?)

After you've done this, let me ask you to do something else: Consider each note in this book as though it were given to you by the Lord—through me—and set your mind on that one thought all day long. Carry it on a card. Put it where you can refer to it. Study it during your quiet time, using cross-references, recording the thoughts that come to you clarifying that one central theme. Cling tenaciously to that ONE word that has come from Him to you in a very special way this day.

Sometimes we can be so close to the mountain, so awed by the immensity of the mass in front of us, so incapacitated because of our emotional involvement, that it is beyond our ability to gain a proper perspective of where we stand.

I do so pray that these notes will provide that perspective, that you will gain new strength, and that they will be a source of encouragement and love for you in your earth-walk with the Lord.

Lovingly,

*Anabel*

# 1

## The Song of My Heart

Lord, when I get up very early in the morning, it is so quiet.

Still.

Then, in the predawn darkness, a soft, melodious anthem begins. It's the cardinal. Now I hear the alto in the cooing of the mourning dove; and of course, the mockingbird comes in with his obbligato.

It seems they start singing praises to You the minute they open their eyes . . . before the first whisper of dawn.

Oh, my dear Father, I want to be a part of their song. I want to praise You with them, to lift my voice with theirs so that others who might be awake can hear and be still . . . and maybe they will want to join the choir, too.

**Let everything alive give praises to the Lord! You praise him!**

PSALM 150:6 TLB

# 2

## Confirm Your Presence, Lord

*Your Father knows what you need, before you ask Him.*

MATTHEW 6:8

*Dear Father,*

*You are aware of everything that is going on in my world at the present time . . . what has happened in the past . . . and what is to come in my future. That is beyond my comprehension.*

*You "know all of my needs before I even tell You about them." That, too, is beyond my comprehension. But I accept it as Truth. I know it. And in spite of that "knowing," I enumerate all of my needs to You time after time. Of course, the presupposition would be that I don't believe You heard me and You're doing nothing about these crises of mine. Well, that's wrong. It's for my own benefit that I present them to You over and over again. I guess I think this will communicate to You how important they are to me. (I am so limited in my understanding of You.)*

Thank You that You have heard me as I talked to You and that You have taken these petitions and You are working Your mighty plan in each of them. In Your timing I will see and understand.

My wisdom is infinitesimally small.
Your wisdom is infinite.
I refuse to tell You WHAT to do . . .
but please confirm to me that You are DOING.

# 3

## An Intimate Moment

Joanna carefully brushed her long, coarse hair before she put the covering over her head. She was scared, yes, but she was so excited! Her hands were trembling as she tucked the vial of perfume into the sleeve of her heavy garment. She was actually going to see Him, maybe even touch Him. And deep within her heart was the hope that He might see her—might notice her in some way. *If I can just get into the portico of Simon's house, surely I can find where they are eating.*

She stayed in the shadows as she walked down the street, fully aware of the people staring and moving away from her as she approached. No one cares to recognize a harlot. But she was used to that. Not that being used to it had taken away the hurt, but she understood. And yet, maybe that humiliating life of sin and degradation was over? Maybe it was behind her? *Maybe He will set me free!*

She had first heard Him the day He taught the multitudes, and had followed Him ever since, sometimes losing herself in the crowds or crouching behind the trees and rocks. There were days when there wasn't anyone around who knew her and she was able to help prepare the meals and serve Him and His disciples.

*There's his house. I know people can hear my heart pounding! Wait, there's the entrance to the servant's quarters. I'll go in there.*

She walked quickly into the dark doorway and then moved toward the sounds of the kitchen.

*I hear Him talking! Oh, please let me be close to Him just this once. I long so to show Him how much I love Him. . . .*

She crept quietly to an open door just behind Jesus. Then, with one deep breath, she stepped into the room, knelt beside Him, and kissed His feet. It was almost funny the way everyone stopped talking and eating. They were shocked—of that there was no doubt—and their silence condemned her.

Joanna wept as she poured the perfume, her tears mingling with the sweet-smelling oil. Then she loosed her hair and began drying those dear, blessed feet.

\* \* \*

Jesus talked to Simon and to the others lounging around the table that day. He talked to Joanna, too. She left, clean and forgiven, knowing that He returned her love and that she was special to Him. We don't hear any more about her, but I want to believe she held steadfastly to her new life.

She made quite a spectacle of herself that day. I can imagine that it took her a long while to make her plans and then to carry them out.

I'm prone to say, "What courage." But no. It wasn't courage that drove Joanna to Simon's house. It was love.

And so the unnamed harlot lives on through biblical history . . . while princes and procurators and scribes and Pharisees, mighty men and strong men and wise men and rich men, are all long since forgotten. Her only claim to fame? She loved much.

*Lord, may I love You as much as Joanna loved You.*

# 4

## *Loving Reminders*

**Then Samuel took a stone and set it between Mizpah and Shen, and named it Ebenezer, saying, "Thus far the Lord has helped us."**

1 SAMUEL 7:12

Ebenezer:
A stone commemorating God's intervention
in very difficult circumstances. Samuel set it there
to be a reminder to him of the presence of God
IN his circumstances.

❉ ❉ ❉

*Lord, I should have some "Ebenezers" stacked around.*

*How far You have come with me—have led me—have helped me. How I thank You for Your loving-kindness, Your compassion, Your patience, Your design for my life.*

*When I look back over the years, Lord, it is absolutely incomprehensible to imagine where I would be if You had not been there to bring me through those difficult circumstances, those stress-filled days.*

Yes, I need an Ebenezer so that when I'm thinking the way is too difficult and I just won't make it, I can turn around and look . . . a rock to remind me: "Thus far the Lord has helped me." Why should I think He has reached a point where He isn't going to be there any longer?

*I'm sorry, dear Lord. I want to learn.*
*Excuse me, please. I have to go find a stone.*

# 5

## The Dwelling Place of God

Before the New Covenant days, it was common knowledge as to where God lived: "in the temple down on the square." He told the people very clearly that this would be His "house."

Then Christ came and walked the narrow streets of Jerusalem, climbed the hills of Israel, and went fishing on the Sea of Galilee. On that catastrophic day when He was crucified, the veil in the temple—behind which God resided—was *ripped* down the middle from top to bottom!

And everyone could see where God had lived.

But He wasn't "homeless" very long. He moved in with me . . . and He moved in with you.

> *Do you not know that you are a temple of God, and that the Spirit of God dwells in you?*
>
> 1 CORINTHIANS 3:16

"But Anabel, that's so . . . well, so . . . *ethereal.* I can't seem to grasp it . . . it eludes me."

Do you know why? It's because you want to *feel* something that would validate it for you. You want to *see* a difference. But Truth is Truth. God cannot lie. And He has said to us, "My Spirit now lives in you. This makes you holy ground, a temple of the living God."

"Wait a minute, Anabel. You're saying I'm 'holy ground'? the 'temple of God' "?

Oh no, *I'm* not, *God* is. You need evidence? All right. Let's look at some verses and discover who you *are* as a Christian and what Christ *is* in your life.

I've written down what each of the following verses says about you. Read it out loud so you can hear what God is saying. And remember, we are not talking about feelings; we're talking about your *true identity.*

| John 1:12 | I am a child of God (Romans 8:16). |
| John 15:1,5 | I am a part of the *true* vine, a channel (branch) of His Life. |
| John 15:15 | I am Christ's friend. |
| John 15:16 | I am chosen and appointed by Christ to bear His fruit. |
| Acts 1:8 | I am a personal witness of Christ for Christ. |
| Romans 3:24 | I have been justified and redeemed. |

| Romans 5:1 | I have been justified (completely forgiven and made righteous) and am at peace with God. |
| --- | --- |
| Romans 6:1–6 | I died with Christ and died to the power of sin's rule in my life. |
| Romans 6:7 | I have been freed from sin's power over me. |
| Romans 6:18 | I am a slave of righteousness. |
| Romans 6:22 | I am enslaved to God. |
| Romans 8:1 | I am forever free from condemnation. |
| Romans 8:14,15 | I am a son of God (God is literally my "Papa") (Galatians 3:26; 4:6). |
| Romans 8:17 | I am an heir of God and fellow heir with Christ. |
| Romans 11:16 | I am holy. |
| Romans 15:7 | Christ has accepted me. |
| 1 Corinthians 1:2 | I have been sanctified. |
| 1 Corinthians 1:30 | I have been placed in Christ by God's doing; Christ is now my wisdom from God, my righteousness, my sanctification, and my redemption. |
| 1 Corinthians 2:12 | I have received the Spirit of God into my life that I might know the things freely given to me by God. |

| 1 Corinthians 2:16 | I have been given the mind of Christ. |
| --- | --- |
| 1 Corinthians 3:16; 6:19 | I am a temple (home) of God; His Spirit (His life) dwells in me. |
| 1 Corinthians 6:17 | I am joined to the Lord and am one spirit with Him. |
| 1 Corinthians 6:19,20 | I have been bought with a price; I am not my own; I belong to God. |
| 1 Corinthians 12:27 | I am a member of Christ's body (Ephesians 5:30). |
| 2 Corinthians 1:21 | I have been established in Christ and anointed by God. |
| 2 Corinthians 2:14 | He always leads me in His triumph in Christ. |
| 2 Corinthians 5:14,15 | Since I have died, I no longer live for myself, but for Christ. |
| 2 Corinthians 5:17 | I am a new creation. |
| 2 Corinthians 5:18,19 | I am reconciled to God and am a minister of reconciliation. |
| 2 Corinthians 5:21 | I am the righteousness of God in Christ. |
| Galatians 2:4 | I have liberty in Christ Jesus. |
| Galatians 2:20 | I have been crucified with Christ, and it is no longer I who live, but Christ lives in me. The life I am now living is Christ's life. |

| Galatians 3:26,28 | I am a child of God and one in Christ. |
| Galatians 4:6,7 | I am a child of God and an heir through God. |
| Ephesians 1:1 | I am a saint (1 Corinthians 1:2; Philippians 1:1; Colossians 1:2). |
| Ephesians 1:3 | I am blessed with every spiritual blessing. |
| Ephesians 1:4 | I was chosen in Christ before the foundation of the world to be holy and without blame before Him. |
| Ephesians 1:7,8 | I have been redeemed and forgiven, and am a recipient of His lavish grace. |
| Ephesians 2:5 | I have been made alive together with Christ. |
| Ephesians 2:6 | I have been raised up and seated with Christ in heaven. |
| Ephesians 2:10 | I am God's workmanship, created in Christ to do His work that He planned beforehand that I should do. |
| Ephesians 2:13 | I have been brought near to God. |
| Ephesians 2:18 | I have direct access to God through the Spirit. |
| Ephesians 2:19 | I am a fellow citizen with the saints and a member of God's household. |

| Ephesians 3:6 | I am a fellow heir, a fellow member of the body, and a fellow partaker of the promise in Christ Jesus. |
| --- | --- |
| Ephesians 3:12 | I may approach God with boldness and confidence. |
| Ephesians 4:24 | I am righteous and holy. |
| Philippians 3:20 | I am a citizen of heaven. |
| Philippians 4:7 | His peace guards my heart and my mind. |
| Philippians 4:19 | God will supply all my needs. |
| Colossians 1:13 | I have been delivered from the domain of darkness and transferred to the kingdom of Christ. |
| Colossians 1:14 | I have been redeemed and forgiven of all my sins. The debt against me has been canceled (Colossians 2:13,14). |
| Colossians 1:27 | Christ Himself is in me. |
| Colossians 2:7 | I have been firmly rooted in Christ and am now being built up and established in Him. |
| Colossians 2:10 | I have been made complete in Christ. |
| Colossians 2:12,13 | I have been buried, raised, and made alive with Christ, and totally forgiven. |

| Colossians 3:1 | I have been raised with Christ. |
| Colossians 3:3 | I have died, and my life is now hidden with Christ in God. |
| Colossians 3:4 | Christ is now my life. |
| Colossians 3:12 | I am chosen of God, holy and dearly loved (1 Thessalonians 1:4). |
| 1 Thessalonians 5:5 | I am a child of light and not of darkness. |
| 2 Timothy 1:7 | I have been given a spirit of power, love, and discipline. |
| 2 Timothy 1:9 | I have been saved and called (set apart) according to God's purpose and grace (Titus 3:5). |
| Hebrews 2:11 | Because I am sanctified and am one with Christ, He is not ashamed to call me His. |
| Hebrews 3:1 | I am a holy partaker of a heavenly calling. |
| Hebrews 3:14 | I am a partaker of Christ. |
| Hebrews 4:16 | I may come boldly before the throne of God to receive mercy and find grace to help in time of need. |
| 1 Peter 2:5 | I am one of God's living stones and am being built up as a spiritual house. |

| 1 Peter 2:9,10 | I am a part of a chosen race, a royal priesthood, a holy nation, a people of God's own possession. |
| --- | --- |
| 1 Peter 2:11 | I am an alien and stranger to this world that I temporarily live in. |
| 1 Peter 5:8 | I am an enemy of the devil. He is my adversary. |
| 2 Peter 1:4 | I have been given God's precious and magnificent promises by which I am a partaker of the divine nature. |
| 1 John 3:1 | God has bestowed a great love on me and called me His child. |
| 1 John 4:15 | God is in me and I am in God. |

This chart is taken from Anabel Gillham, *The Confident Woman* (Eugene, OR: Harvest House Publishers, 1993), pp. 72–76.

Now, even though you may not "feel" like these verses are true, are they in fact true? Yes. Why? Because God said so. You, then, must accept His Word and *act* like what He has called you: a wonderful new creation! The very dwelling place of God!

* * *

We are so uninhibited as children. How well I remember dancing on my front porch, pretending I was Ginger Rogers. It didn't matter how many people went by. As far as *I* was concerned, when they looked at me *they were seeing Ginger:* long blonde hair (pageboy style), willowy, graceful, and beautiful. But I was just "pretending."

When we "act out" Jesus living through us—in us— we are *not* pretending. It is truth! But the people who are watching will see the grace and beauty of Him "dancing" through us. How we cheat ourselves every day when we say, "This is too difficult for me to understand . . . too mystical. I just can't do it."

*Come on. Let's go out on the front porch and dance!*

# 6

## *From Trash to Treasure*

The latest acquisition that made its way into our garage came from the curb over by Eddie and Gina's yard. We beat the trash truck to it.

It used to be a Victrola (for those of you old enough to know what a Victrola is), but the lid had been permanently fastened down *after* about a foot of the cabinet itself had been sawed off. Surprisingly, though, it was a pretty good sawing job.

The insides had been confiscated about the turn of the century (you may detect a tad of sarcasm in that statement), so there was a hollow cavern spattered with glue; there were nail holes everywhere; the sides were splintered and the bottom was shaky. Bill saw great potential for that sorry piece of wood, and he elected *me* to bring it out—*thanks, Honey.*

How many tired, sad-looking (sometimes hopeless-looking) pieces of furniture have I taken under my wing to make presentable? or even lovely? or *just like new?* And every time I start another one I say to Bill (and he reminds me that I've said it before), "Why I ever start a project like this is beyond me! Completely beyond me. I don't like to do it. It's messy. And who can guarantee what it will turn out like? Why do I do it?"

I've not ruined one yet, but of course there's a first time for everything. Yet I always start by closing my eyes and heaving a heavy sigh. Then, with great determination, I attack—just like I knew exactly what I was doing!

But I've learned some rather nice lessons while my hands are getting shriveled and the gnats are buzzing around my ears. The Lord uses practical things to teach us practical things.

Just suppose that I undertake an old oak desk that is really going to be beautiful, but I mess up. Not just a little bit. A *large* bit. And the piece is ruined.

*You, Lord, have the capability of undoing all my blemishes and mistakes, of taking me back to bare wood again. Better still, You are able to take my gouges and stains—my flaws—and rub and polish them until they're really the prettiest areas on the desk!*

*You have done this in my life so many times. I show up in Your garage a mess, but You always see the potential. I wonder if You heave a sigh and, with great determination, begin the project?*

*That I don't know. One thing I do know: that You are working; that You are the epitome of patience; that You are skilled—the very best—at refinishing sorry things that might be on the curb ready for the trash truck.*

*How can I ever thank You for what You have done for me? I can't. It's impossible. But You know my thoughts, my heart, the depth of my gratitude. And You see my potential.*

**I will give thanks to Thee, for I am fearfully and wonderfully made . . .**

PSALM 139:14

# 7

## The Keeper of the Keys

*God sent Him . . . to proclaim liberty to captives, and freedom to prisoners.*

**ISAIAH 61:1**

Just imagine . . .
  slowly now . . .

  having your hair done. You're sitting under the dryer.
  Sauntering down the walkways at the mall, leisurely.
  Going down an escalator.
  Sitting on the bed and taking off your shoes.
  Unzipping your coat—it's an ankle-length coat.
  Carrying a gallon jug of milk in your right hand.
  Carrying a heavy chain in your right hand. It goes up
      and over your shoulder. It's fastened around
      your neck.

*Here's a key to the lock.* "Thank you." Unlock the padlock.
    Take off the chain. There's a marker on it, a tag,
    and something is written on it: FEAR.

Now there's a chain around your ankle, a heavy one. You
    have to drag it as you walk.

23

Someone hands you a key. Use it. What does the tag say?

    LONELINESS.

You never realized! Another chain! ANGER. You turn and look for the Person with the keys. There He is. Ask Him if He has one for ANGER. As He hands you the key you notice that His hand is slightly deformed. It's an ugly scar, right in the middle of His hand.

Where is your coat—that long one? There it is. Slip into it. It covers you completely. Zip it. All the way up. Wait. It isn't a coat. It is Jesus Christ. How good this feels to be enveloped in this love. This softness. This warmth.

*Anabel, I came to set you free. Let Me.*

# 8

## Just Because You're Mine

Mace could sing one song with great gusto—just one: Jesus Loves Me.

> *Jesus loves me, this I know,*
> *For the Bible tells me so.*
> *Little ones to Him belong,*
> *They are weak but He is strong.*

He would throw his head back and hold on to that first "Yes" in the chorus as long as he could, and then he would get tickled and almost fall out of his chair.

Sometimes—when I think back on those days that seem so long ago—*I can still hear him giggle.* How special that memory is to me. . . .

I never doubted for a moment that Jesus loved our profoundly retarded little boy. It didn't matter that he would never sit with the kids in the back of the church and, on a certain special night, walk down the aisle, take the pastor by the hand, and invite Jesus into his heart. It was entirely irrelevant that he could not quote a single verse of Scripture, that he would never be able to reason or to comprehend God's love, that he would never be a dad—I *knew* that Jesus loved Mason.

What I could not comprehend, what I could not accept, was that Jesus could love Mason's mother, Anabel. I believed that in order for anyone to accept me, to love me, I had to perform for them. My standard for getting love was performance-based, so I performed constantly, perfectly. And I was convinced that if anyone ever *really* got to know me, he or she wouldn't like me.

Mace could never have performed for anyone's love . . . but oh, how we loved him. His condition eventually deteriorated to such a degree—and so rapidly—that we had to institutionalize him when he was very young, so we enrolled him in the Enid State School for Mentally Handicapped Children.

We drove regularly the 120 miles to see him, but on this particular weekend he was at home for a visit. He had been with us since Thursday evening, and it was now Saturday afternoon. As soon as the dinner dishes were done, I would gather his things together and take him back to *his* house. I had done this many times before, but today God had something in mind that would change my life forever.

As I was washing the dishes, Mason was sitting in his chair watching me, or at least he was looking at me. That's when it began—spinning emotions, tumbling stomach, the familiar sickening thoughts of separation and defeat: *In just a little while, I'm going to start packing Mason's toys and his clothes, and take him away again. I can't do that. I simply cannot do it.* I stopped washing dishes and got down on my knees in front of

Mace. I took his dirty little hands in mine and tried desperately to reach him.

"Mason, I love you. I love you. If only you could understand how much I love you."

He just stared. He couldn't understand; he didn't comprehend. I stood up and started washing dishes again, but that didn't last long. This sense of urgency, almost panic, came over me, and once more I dried my hands and knelt in front of my precious little boy.

"My dear Mason, if only you could say to me, 'I love you, Mother.' I *need* that, Mace."

Nothing.

I stood up to the sink again. More dishes, more washing, more crying. But now thoughts, foreign to my way of thinking, began filtering into my conscious awareness. I believe God spoke to me that day, and this is what He said: "Anabel, you don't look at your son and turn away in disgust because he's sitting there with saliva drooling out of his mouth; you don't shake your head, repulsed because he has dinner all over his shirt or because he's sitting in a dirty, smelly diaper when he ought to be able to take care of himself. Anabel, you don't reject Mason because all the dreams you had for him have been destroyed. You don't reject him because he doesn't *perform* for you. You love him, Anabel, *just because he is yours*. Mason doesn't willfully reject your love, but you willfully reject Mine. I love you, Anabel, not because you're neat or attractive, not because you do things well, not because you *perform* for Me—I love you *just because you're Mine."*

Incredible! Unbelievable! I had struggled for so many years, hating my performance patterns and yet living to perform, driven to perform, searching out the praise of people and thirsting for the love of God that I thought could come only to those who performed well enough to merit it. Yet God had just shown me that He loved me in spite of anything and everything, and He had shown me in a way that I could understand—through my dear, sweet Mason.

Do you understand? You don't have to do anything for Him; you don't have to be something for Him. You can know that there is Someone who loves you not because of the way you do or don't look, or because of the talents you do or don't have. All you have to do is accept it: He loves you *just because you are His.*

\* \* \*

Well, that's not the end of Mason's story. It wasn't long after that Sunday with him that Bill, our son Preston, and I went to visit him in Enid. We held his hand, stroked his hair, and talked to him. And then we prayed. *God, by Your grace we've lived victoriously and have used Mace's little life and influence for Your glory . . . but we feel that he has suffered enough and that all the influence for Christ that can be realized from his life has pretty well been exhausted. God, if it be Your will, we ask that you take him to be with You.*

We kissed Mason goodbye and headed home. It was the very next morning when the school called to say that Mason had "unexpectedly passed away during the night"—and we knew that he had slipped away to be with Jesus.

The Far East Broadcasting Company in Cheju, Korea, received a letter from Bill a short time later: " . . . there was some insurance money. It belongs to God. We pass it along to FEBC for use in the China-Cheju Island project. . . ."

Mason's gift helped build a transmitter building for the 250,000-watt radio signal that now beams the gospel of Christ to China, Russia, and Japan. And it is because of Mason that people will continue to learn of Jesus, of His saving grace . . . and of the fact that He loves us *just because we are His.*

> *Yes, <u>Jesus</u> loves me . . .*
> *Yes, Jesus <u>loves</u> me . . .*
> *Yes, Jesus loves <u>me</u> . . .*
> *The Bible tells me so.*

# 9

## A Childlike Heart

*Truly I say to you, whoever does not receive the kingdom of God like a child shall not enter it at all.*

**MARK 10:15**

*How would a child come to God?*

With *no* reservations, no preconceived fears or doubts.

"Looking up" to Him—from a child's perspective.
*He is big and I am little. He is strong. I am weak.*
*He will hold me in His arms. He will hold my hand.*
*He will know what to do. . . .*

Ready to listen and to ask questions,
but not to express her views or to argue
with Him about His views.

Giving Him the responsibility of caring for her.
Indeed, *expecting* Him to care for her.
Trusting Him to care for her.

Reaching out to touch Him. Holding His hand for
security and comfort.

Resting in His lap.
Putting her arms around His neck.
Being excited to see Him and be with Him.
Knowing that He is wiser than she is.
Knowing that He is stronger than she is.

I have often thought that the time to enjoy your child to the fullest is when she, with childlike trust and love . . .

walks by your side
holds your hand
wants to be with you, near you
listens to what you say
believes what you tell her
looks to you every day to plan her life
asks permission to do something her way
brings her problems to you
enjoys the "little" things you give her
appreciates the "little" things you do for her
doesn't question your decisions
doesn't need anyone in her life but you
lets you know that you are the most important
    person in her life.

*Dear Lord, why do we grow away from You*
*as we get older? Why do we begin to think*
*we don't need You? Why do we question*
*Your motives? Your love? Your power?*
*I am so sorry, Lord God.*
*How I need You.*
*In childlike faith I come to You today,*
*recognizing that You are my Father, my God . . .*
*and that I am Your child.*

# 10

## *Close to the Father*

He was traveling on a bus in Israel and, as would be expected, his comprehension of the conversations going on all around him was limited, to say the least. And then a man boarded with his son.

He was a little child, and he crawled up into his daddy's lap for the ride. They started laughing and playing together. And then the little boy reached up, took hold of his daddy's beard, and started shaking it kind of like a wet dog shakes, and he was saying, *"Abba Abba Abba"*—a word our friend understood.

Do you know what *Abba* means? It's the Greek word for "Father." It "approximates to a personal name," kind of like "Papa." It is "the word framed by the lips of infants" and by older children "expressing [their] love and intelligent confidence" in their father.*

Jesus came, talking to God and about God. But He didn't call Him *Jehovah.* Or *Elohim.* Or *Adonai.* Or *El Shaddai.* Or any other of the names that the people

---

*W.E. Vine, *Expository Dictionary of New Testament Words* (Nashville, TN: Nelson, n.d.).

called God. No, Jesus came and called Him *Abba*, Papa, Daddy, Father.

In the book of Matthew, Jesus addresses God 43 times as Father. He took an awesome God, a fearful God, an unapproachable God, a God who was known to strike out when He was not obeyed, the God of the Old Testament . . . and He introduced us to a loving Father.

How we have structured and formalized (and, in so doing, ostracized) the Father that Jesus wanted us to know! For our conversation with Him to be "pleasing," we have been told we must "look just right," assume just the right posture, be in the right place at the right time, say just the right things, use the prerequisite Thee's and Thou's—and that only then will He *really* consider honoring our prayers.

\* \* \*

*Oh, God! Dear heavenly Father. That we would build such ominous barriers separating us from You, making You into the untouchable God of Eli and Jeremiah. You are our Father. You love us. You care for us. You don't want to see us hurt. You have given us everything that we need to live here in this world of godlessness. A world that has no use for You. A world where evil and cruel people hurt and maim and kill. A world where Your creation is crying out for release from the bondage of sin.*

*Jesus didn't approach You as "Almighty God," though that is who You are.*

*He didn't approach You as* El Elyon, *the Most High, though that is who You are.*

*He didn't approach You as* Jehovah Jireh, *though that is who You are.*

*He approached You as Your Son, Your beloved Child.*

*And He called You . . . Abba.*

**For you have not received**
**a spirit of slavery leading to fear again,**
**but you have received a spirit of adoption**
**    as sons**
**by which we cry out, "Abba! Father!"**

ROMANS 8:15

**And because you are sons,**
**God has sent forth the Spirit of His Son**
**into our hearts, crying, "Abba! Father!"**

GALATIANS 4:6

# 11

## *Our Time Together*

**So let us know, let us press on to know the Lord. His going forth is as certain as the dawn, And He will come to us like the rain, Like the spring rain watering the earth.**

**HOSEA 6:3**

*Lord, I want to talk with You this morning.*

*The verse says that Your "going forth" is as certain as the dawn, so I'm confident that You're here with me. And this bare winter ground is ready to drink in the early rain with a soft, pliable heart—and with her face upturned.*

*Your Word tells me that You know my every thought, so You must be available to me. You're ready to converse with me on a lot of subjects that no one knows about except You—very personal, very deep subjects that I wouldn't want to share with anyone else. You know what I'm thinking. You know what I would like to say but can't. You know why I'm hesitant to bring up certain thoughts. You know me.*

*The question I'm concerned about is this: Am I available to You? Do I know You well enough to talk with You?*

*Well, Your Word is You. Your thoughts, written down. But sometimes You place a distinct thought between the lines and say to me, "Do you understand this verse, Anabel? Let Me explain it to you." Or, "Can You see this from My perspective?"*

*Sometimes You draw a mental picture for me that opens a file I had never thought of opening, making a passage relevant to me and to my world— now. How I love for You to do that . . . and I start cross-referencing, probing, finding out what Your thoughts are about the subject, getting to know You a little better.*

*I really don't want to spend our time together telling You about all my problems and making suggestions as to how You should take care of them. You know my needs before I even ask.*

*No, this time is just for You and for me. I want to know You, Lord. I want to be able to converse with You on some of Your favorite topics. Please talk to me. I love being with You and listening to Your voice.*

*And thank You, Lord Jesus, for making this awesome,*
*powerful, infinite, all-knowing God*
*an approachable Father.*

# 12

## *Undoing the Deceiver*

I could do that, too . . . it wouldn't *hurt* anything . . .
*No, I shouldn't.*
But why not?
*It's wrong.*
Who says it's wrong?
*I would hate myself afterwards.*
But I'd have such a good time . . .

It wouldn't hurt to lie just a tad . . .
*I'd get caught.*
Lots of people juggle the totals, though . . .
*That doesn't make it right.*
Who says?
*Well . . .*
I don't think anyone would ever find out . . .

Both of these voices sound very familiar . . . *wait a minute.* They sound like—why—both of them sound just like me! What's going on? Are there two "me's"?

Voices. *Two voices.*

One voice urges me to do the right thing. The Christlike thing. The good thing. The thing of integrity.

The other one urges me to do just the opposite. It makes light of being truthful or good or pure, and it certainly doesn't want to be labeled a "religious, Bible-totin' fanatic." Integrity isn't even in its vocabulary.

*And the lights get a little brighter.* I begin—just begin—to see what Paul was talking about in Romans 7:21–23: "I find then the principle that evil is present in me, the one who wishes to do good. For I joyfully concur with the law of God in the inner man, but I see a different law in the members of my body, waging war against the law of my mind, and making me a prisoner of the law of sin which is in my members."

To Paul it is a foregone conclusion—*without a doubt*—that as a Christian I am a new creature in Christ Jesus (2 Corinthians 5:17). A new creation! Me, "the one who wishes to do good," who "joyfully concur[s] with the law of God in the inner man"! I am a person who wishes to do the right thing not only because I think God's laws are good and just and right, but because those very laws are written on my heart and in my mind (Hebrews 10:16).

But Paul also says there is something in my *body*—"in the members of my body"—that "wages battle" against my mind, my mind that wants to do good, my mind that is "the mind of Christ" (1 Corinthians 2:16). It's a power called "sin," he says, and because of it I often "practice the very evil that I do not wish."

But how can I do hurtful, mean, thoughtless, selfish things and yet be a new creature in Christ at the same time? What's wrong here? *Something unusual is going on.* . . . Why do I wind up doing the very thing I don't want to do—sinning?

*Because I am deceived.*

John called Satan the one "who deceives the whole world" (Revelation 12:9). Satan is the Deceiver, and he deceives us, the new creations in Christ, the ones who want to do good. Now read this carefully: The power of sin is the messenger boy who carries out the Deceiver's battle strategy in this war being waged against the law of our minds. And here is how he does it. . . .

The Deceiver's game plan hinges on deception, and his goal is to keep us from experiencing the life that is ours in Christ, to prevent us at any cost from realizing true peace and victory. For example, I shared with you earlier some verses (facts) from God's Word concerning your true identity and the power of Christ which lives within you. I have told you that these facts will literally revolutionize your life if you appropriate them.

The Deceiver doesn't want you to appropriate them, to take them for your own use. He doesn't want you to walk in these truths. They will bring peace and joy into your life. They will bring you victory. So he wars against the law of your mind, and he does this through your thought-life. His access to your thought-life? Why, through the power of sin "in the members of [your] body." *And he operates by giving you thoughts, almost always with first-person, singular pronouns—I, me, my, myself, and mine.*

These thoughts will be disguised as the way you've always thought, and the Deceiver's success comes when you, because the thoughts are so familiar, so "like you," *accept* these thoughts as your own. Then and only then does he have you—and you wind up doing what you hate. *Thinking* what you hate. *Believing* what you hate.

Do you see that if you're not aware of his game plan you'll listen to him and he can convince you of anything? Adultery. Hopelessness. Materialism. Chronic depression. Even suicide. He can convince you that the old you wasn't really crucified with Christ at all when you asked Him into your heart (Galatians 2:20), or that she has come back to life again: "I'm not a new person! I only have to look at all the garbage in my life to know that. New creation—ha! I don't even read the Bible that much. I'm not good at my job and I'm not a good wife— I'm more of an embarrassment to my family than anything else. Everyone would be better off without me. . . ."

Examine those statements carefully. Do you see the pronouns? I, my, me. My dear one, *these are not your thoughts.* A new creation, one with the very mind of Christ, does not—indeed *cannot*—generate such thoughts. *You are not fighting a civil war—the good you against the bad you.* No, it's you—the "righteousness of God in Christ" (2 Corinthians 5:21)—against "the power of sin waging war against the law of [your] mind and making [you] a prisoner of the law of sin which is in [your] members"!

Now, if you are not responsible for generating these thoughts, where does your accountability come in? When *are you* responsible? "Do not let sin reign in your mortal body" (Romans 6:12). It's all in the *letting.* If you choose with your free will to accept the thoughts submitted by the Deceiver through the power of sin, taking them in *as though they were your own,* then they become your thoughts and you are responsible for sinning.

My dear one, I know this can seem confusing. But seek Him. Study these pages and put these truths to the test. In these brief paragraphs we have exposed the Deceiver and how he works. We now have the information necessary to intercept his passes. Oh, please understand that you do not have to accept these thoughts any longer. *You are a beautiful new creature in Christ,* and He longs for you to allow Him to love you, to heal you, to enable you to overcome your past and face your todays and tomorrows—to *live*!

You see, if you accept this simple theology, you'll know what to listen for and how to determine where the thoughts are coming from. And you can say, "No! I refuse to let that thought set up shop in my mind!" Obviously you can't stop the thoughts from coming, but you certainly *can* stop them from unpacking their suitcases and putting down their bedrolls. So you slam the door and turn up the music so you won't hear him knock again, and you start singing. (The power of sin doesn't like to sing praise songs.) You set your mind on the things God tells you to think about—Him, mainly.

You know what will happen? The thought will begin to subside. It will begin to go away. Oh sure, it will probably come back later on, but you will actually have won a battle! You'll know how it feels to win instead of always losing. In this there is *great* hope.

After all, that is why He came to us in the first place:

*"I know the plans that I have for you,"*
*declares the Lord, "plans for welfare*
*and not for calamity, to give you a future*
*and a hope."*

JEREMIAH 29:11

*Which voice is really yours?*

# 13

## *Nothing Can Separate Us*

*I am convinced that neither death, nor
life, nor angels, nor principalities, nor
things present, nor things to come, nor
powers, nor height, nor depth, nor any
other created thing shall be able to separate us from the love of God, which is in
Christ Jesus our Lord.*

ROMANS 8:38,39

That pretty well covers the "waterfront," doesn't it?
There isn't anything that could come into my life that
would not fall into one of those categories. What happens
in *death*—a fearful thought not only for myself, but for
the people God gave me and who move around in my circle of love. What happens in *life*—tragedies, disappointments, pain, grief, any circumstance that comes my way.
They are all on the list.

And yet that just *doesn't work for me. It's not always true in my life.*

There *are* times when I'm separated from God. When
I *feel* lonely and misunderstood. When I'm discouraged and

disappointed in my marriage. When I *feel* like I'm facing life all by myself, and there's no one to listen or to care. So I'm depressed. When I *feel* like I've had more than my share of this world's problems, and I really expected and asked for so little. When I *feel* resentment. And as far as *feeling* like God's love is something that just can't be taken from me? I'm smart enough to know that God can't *always* love someone who does the things I sometimes do. That's just the way I *feel* about it. *Sigh.*

\* \* \*

*Feelings! Feelings! Feelings!*

Depression. Resentment. Loneliness. Discouragement. Anger. Inadequacy. Bitterness. *Ad infinitum!*

Why do I allow my feelings to control my mind when they don't even have the capacity to THINK? or REASON?

It's as though I lose the power to choose, to remember, to observe, to logically deduce, to use my God-given ability to think and reason, to accept and rest in Truth—I let how I feel dictate to me what I "know"! How foolish of me. How shallow. How wrong!

*Lord, if none of the horrible things in this world can separate You from me or me from You—no, that isn't right . . . I must rephrase that. I'll start over.*

> *Lord,* since *none of these things*
> *have the power to separate us,*
> *why do I allow my*
> <u>feelings</u>
> *to come between us?*

# 14

## *A New Definition of New*

*"New"* doesn't always mean improved, does it?

Corrie Ten Boom started a *new* life when she walked through the door of the concentration camp.

Joni Eareckson Tada started a *new* life the moment her head hit that hidden rock at the bottom of the lake.

Mother started a *new* life the afternoon she found Dad in his favorite chair out on the side lawn . . . the still-warm yet lifeless victim of a massive coronary.

Pat started a *new* life on Saturday morning at 9:30 when her husband announced that he was filing for divorce . . . "and there isn't anything to discuss."

Janie started a *new* life when the doctor told her, "I can't give you a date. All I can tell you is that you don't have long to live and that there's going to be some intense suffering ahead for you."

Anabel started a *new* life that day in the doctor's office when he announced, "Your son is incurably ill and will be hopelessly retarded."

* * *

This "new" simply means something you have not experienced before, and I'm quite sure that some of you are experiencing a *new* life this very day—or someone dear to you is painfully changing from the old to the new. I also know that some of the adjectives attached to this new life are not at all pretty:

*Lonely* . . . I'm all by myself.

*Weary* . . . I'm so tired.

*Empty* . . . There's a void, I have no purpose.

*Frustrating* . . . I feel so utterly defeated.

*Hurting* . . . I had no idea how painful this would be.

*Hopeless* . . . It's too hard—I'm emotionally drained and stressed out.

*Fearful* . . . I'm scared—I don't know where I'm going.

*Discouraged* . . . What do I do? How do I keep on? I just can't do it.

*Sorrowful* . . . It seems like grief has enveloped me—I can't remember pleasant times, and I wonder if I'll ever be happy again.

There are times when my emotions have been so very high that remembering or reasoning or studying were virtually impossible; and if not impossible, something that I just couldn't settle down to do at that point in my life.

There have been times when I have been so close to the mountain, so overwhelmed by the immensity of the mass in front of me, so incapacitated because of my emotional involvement,

that it has been beyond my ability to gain a proper perspective of where I'm standing.

Then is when I must *force* myself to remember:

My circumstances have changed, but my God has not changed.

He is as close to me today as He was yesterday.

He still loves me more than I can possibly comprehend.

He still lives within me to meet this tragic, difficult circumstance for me and through me.

I will not be destroyed if I will only let Him face each second, each moment of each day in His strength, since mine is gone.

I cannot understand His ways. I do not know what He is planning. But I do know His heart. He loves me.

※ ※ ※

I would like to help . . . please let me.
These simple words that you read each day—
hold on to them tenaciously,
set your mind on *them,*
not on your emotions or your circumstances.
*I love you.*

# 15

## *His Love for Me*

Jesus Christ is in my life . . .
    there is no other.
The thought of
spending a single day
outside His love
    His gentleness
    His tenderness
    His understanding
    His power
is not only frightening
it causes me to despair
to become weak with hopelessness.

How could I ever meet "today"
    if I had to do it alone?
For not only do I draw from His strength
    but I grasp for His
    faithfulness to me
    His complete acceptance of me
    the peace that I find only in His presence.

For, you see, I've come to accept myself because of
Him.
      I find that I do those things
      which are kind and good
      loving others
      while I bask in His love for me!

All I am or ever hope to be
      lies in Him.
      Without Him—I am nothing.
      With Him—I am everything.
            And when I am not "everything"
            He loves me still.

# 16

## The Master's Voice

Dad loved to fly fish, and it wasn't necessary for him to have a friend along. He thrived on the solitude, the quietness, the beauty, the "swish" of the line from his reel, seeing how close he could put his fly to "that dark shadow under the tree across the river—they'll be hiding in the shade by that stump." They? The bluegill. The goggle-eyed perch. The smaller fish, but real fighters. You *knew* when one was on your line!

He had gone to Blackfork and was heading home . . . alone. The roads were made for four-wheel drive vehicles and would have been an exciting challenge, but four-wheelers weren't around when Dad was here, so he drove the old black Pontiac slowly, carefully, lingering, still enjoying his own private forest.

It was then that he spotted the deserted campsite. There was a cleared place where the tent had been staked, a deep hole that had been used for ice, and a burned-out campfire. And there was something else—a little black-and-brown dog sitting forlornly and expectantly by the pile of rocks that had bordered the fire.

Dad got out and made friends with the dog, sizing up the situation pretty quickly. The dog had no doubt been exploring and wasn't around when time came to break camp and head home. (I can imagine how they had waited and hoped and whistled and called and finally left . . . without him.) It seemed like the dog knew that Dad was his last chance, so he hopped into the car and they headed for Poteau together.

We were "dogless" at the time (a rarity), so seeing the lost dog in Daddy's arms was a real thrill for us. He was a small terrier with wiry black hair and tan feet. His tail hadn't been bobbed and the tip was tan like his feet. With his ears up, he was not over a foot tall. He let us hold him and love him, sensing perhaps that this was going to be his new home. We tried every name that we could think of, but we just couldn't excite him. He answered best to a two-syllable name, so we finally called him Sonny.

Dad put an ad in the *LeFlore County Sun:* "Dog found at campsite on south end of Blackfork River. Call 410 to identify." When a call would come, he would always ask the caller to describe his or her dog, but Sonny never fit the bill. We were *so* glad, because he had won our hearts. His master had obviously spent time playing with him and training him; one of his favorite pastimes was knocking a pop bottle around with his nose and playing with it like a ball. Sonny had accepted us and we had accepted Sonny. He was part of the Hoyle family.

Then one day Dad called to say, "Honey, we've got a young man here who thinks the little dog is his. I'm sending him out to let him see Sonny."

I was at home by myself and didn't know quite how I could face someone coming and claiming Sonny, taking him away. I put him on the back porch and closed the kitchen door.

Our front door opened into a hallway. The first door on the right was to our guest bedroom, the immediate left to the living room. The living room and dining room were one large, long room, with a door at the end of the dining area that opened into the kitchen; the door to the back porch was in line with that door. The divan had been placed as a divider between the two areas. Sonny could go *around* the divan or crawl *under* it, but it was too high for him to go over.

A knock on the front door. I didn't want to go. I dreaded it, but knew I had to. The young man at the door stood on crutches—you could tell they had been his life-long companions. He introduced himself and I ushered him into the living room—right at the front end by the piano. We talked a moment, then I suggested that he call the dog when I opened the door to the back porch so we could see what kind of response he would get. He agreed. When I opened the door, Sonny was playing with a pop bottle.

Suddenly there was a short, clear whistle and a call: "Patrick!"

Sonny froze and tilted his head to one side, the abandoned pop bottle rolling toward the wall. Then again, the whistle and that name, "Patrick!"

Patrick scratched at the linoleum floor with his little short legs, trying to get traction, and then he started running—through the dining table legs, *over the top* of the divan and, with one wild leap, into the outstretched arms of his master, who was ready... balanced... watching anxiously with tears on his cheeks. He grabbed that little dog and held him so close and tight! Patrick knew his master's voice.

\* \* \*

I hope I did justice to that story. It's one of my favorites. Why did I tell it? Because I want to talk about who we are and who God is. We are Patrick, and we have a Master who loves us more than we can possibly comprehend. Oh, Patrick was surviving with us, but his heart was still with the person who loved him, played with him, trained him, and drove 160 miles over a crooked, narrow road to claim him and identify him as his own.

Do you *know* who you are? Do you know that those arms are outstretched, that He is standing and waiting, with a tear-streaked face, for you to run and with "one, wild leap" jump into His arms? Do you know that you are totally and completely loved? Oh, you may be surviving in your present surroundings, entertaining yourself with your "pop bottle," but are you separated from the One who loves you so much that He gave His life for you?

Knowing who you are brings a confidence into your life that cannot be taken away. Jesus got down on His knees, on the floor, and washed the feet of the disciples. How could He humble Himself to that degree? Well, John 13:3 tells us: "Jesus, *knowing* that the Father had given all things into His hands, and that He had come forth from God, and was going back to God. . . ." Jesus *knew* two things: 1) who He was; and 2) that He was passionately loved by His Father.

You may label yourself an engineer, a librarian, a business mogul, a student, an accomplished vocalist, a devoted mother, a retired banker, an executive secretary, or a wife above reproach. Any of those things could be gone in the twinkling of an eye. Now, *who are you?* There is only one identity that is unshakable; one identity that is for eternity; one identity that will never fail you. *That is your identity in Christ.*

Patrick's story has limits, I know. It's a sweet little dog story, more for children than for mature adults. But are you sure you know what the story is saying? Perhaps you need to become "like a little child." And don't look at the obvious limits; look at the incredible possibilities. Patrick knew *his* master. Patrick knew who *he* was. That filled his heart with joy, his life with purpose.

Whatever you have in your hands, let it go. Then kind of tilt your head and listen. Did you hear that whistle? Sharp. Clear. And you recognize the voice, don't you? Okay. Start scrambling. Run. Faster. Go under and over the obstacles, no matter how tall they seem to be. Then jump! He's watching . . . He's able to catch you . . . and His arms will gather you close and hold you, and you'll be back where you belong.

# 17

## Teach Me, Lord

Timothy, my beloved son, remember that . . .

*All scripture is inspired by God and profitable for teaching, for reproof, for correction, for training in righteousness, that the man of God may be adequate, equipped for every good work.*

Grace be with you,
Paul

**2 TIMOTHY 3:16,17**

*Teaching.* It informs me. It sorts out my thoughts. It helps me to determine and clarify what I believe. I went to college to learn about a certain field—art. And I remember it being so interesting and fascinating to me. I was excited about what I was going to learn, who the teacher was going to be, how many hours I would chalk up on my transcript, and how it would all mesh with my dreams and goals.

This same excitement should really be a part of my Bible study. The Teacher is interesting, well-qualified, fascinating. The hours transfer quite nicely, and my pursuit of the field definitely enhances my dreams and goals.

*Reproof.* This means rebuke. This means to be critical. This is how I recognize sin in my life.

God's reproof is always a *constructive,* critical evaluation. "He whose ear listens to the life-giving reproof will dwell among the wise" (Proverbs 15:31); "He who hates reproof is stupid" (12:1); "Whom the Lord loves He reproves" (3:12).

I certainly don't want to be classified as "stupid," as a hardhead who refuses constructive correction. I am confident of His love for me, and I also recognize Him as the source of wisdom. So I listen. I ponder. I accept reproof.

How thankful I am that there is Someone who has the courage to point to my poor performance and tell me that I'm blowing it! That's reproof. Just think, for example, how tragic it would be to go through your entire stay on planet Earth offending, hurting, alienating people through your poor behavior . . . and have no one to point it out to you. Oh my, yes! Reproof is very definitely profitable.

*Correction.* This tells me *how* to change. Change must be necessary, or the reproof would not have come in the first place.

If I need to change, to correct the way I have been doing something, then the proper or right way to do it must be provided for me. With hope. With kindness. With tact. And with *encouragement,* which is the fertilizer for correction.

*Training in righteousness.* Training is the "how to" of applying the reproof and correction. Training means involvement. Apprenticeship. The actual "doing," learning by experience. I need "hands-on" experience. I need to know firsthand the "right" way (God's way) to face life, to face my circumstances. I need to know how to "respond" instead of "react." I need to know how to practice discernment instead of acquiescing to depression. I want to learn how to walk under "Christ-control" instead of self-control. This is the goal, the attainable dream.

And He shows me how to do this as I spend time with Him, study His teachings, His life, His message . . . as I live with Him, sensing His peace, His training—and all toward teaching me how to live and behave as the righteous new person He has created and rebirthed me to be.

❖ ❖ ❖

*Lord, when I sit down to read the Scriptures, I'm taking care to meet a very important need in my day, in my life. I'm taking care to attend class, to concentrate on my goals and dreams—Your goals and dreams for me.*

**You call Me Teacher and Lord, and you are right, for so I am.**

**JOHN 13:13**

*Lord, teach me.*

# 18

## Sweet and Sour Chicken

Betty, my sis, is a gourmet cook. As I look back on our growing-up days, I can see that I was much more willing to dust and mop and clean out drawers than to spend time in the kitchen. Maybe that's why she's a gourmet cook and I'm still dusting and mopping and cleaning out drawers!

She has a recipe for sweet and sour chicken that is *out* of this world—simply delicious. The night she prepared it for Bill and me I asked for the recipe and copied it on the spot. When I got home, I very promptly and neatly placed it in its proper category in my recipe box— and then just as promptly forgot it.

I had tasted it. I knew it was wonderful. I had the instructions so I could try my hand at turning out something just as wonderful. But I knew the simple secret lay in *doing* it. I was going to have to get out my recipe, probably call Bet to be sure I copied everything just right, and then undertake the project. And I'd be so pleased, and so would everyone else who put their feet under the table—*hopefully!*

This is the way I sometimes handle spiritual "dishes" that I've tasted. I know they're wonderful, good, profitable, and possible—and that it's all in the *doing*.

I came across the following study analysis somewhere. It applies here.

> We will retain 5 to 10 percent of what we hear.
> We will retain 30 percent of what we read.
> We will retain 50 percent of what we hear and read.
> We will retain 90 percent of what we hear, read, and do.

I bet that somewhere between the 50 and 90 percent we could place "writing it down." *Doing,* of course, is the most effective learning process. *Writing down* the method of accomplishment, the success or failure of the procedure, etc., will increase our understanding, give fingertip access to notes, and record our perception, appropriation, and commitment levels.

So let's add that to our analysis: *We will retain 75 percent of what we hear, read and write.*

※ ※ ※

Well, after years of eating sweet and sour chicken at the local Chinese restaurant, I finally tried *my* hand at the dish. Did I have to talk myself into this gourmet endeavor? Yes. I had all kinds of excuses as to why I couldn't do it. Time consuming? Yes—all afternoon to put it together. Concentrated effort? Yes. Worth it all? Yes. No one really praises me for the clean-drawer routine, but the praise was hot and heavy that night at the supper table.

And so it goes with the seminar I attend, the sermon or tape I hear, the book I read. I know that the truth I've tasted is wonderful, good, profitable, and possible. . . .

But does it take discipline? Yes.
And does it take time? Yes.
Is there work involved? Yes.
And is it worth the effort? Yes.

*Be diligent to present yourself approved to God as a workman who does not need to be ashamed, handling accurately the word of truth.*

2 Timothy 2:15

# 19

## *What Is God Saying to You?*

Are you familiar with Luke chapter 15? The lost sheep. The lost coin. The prodigal son and his father . . . You've no doubt heard many sermons on these passages (with as many different interpretations and lessons!). Voices of authority have influenced you—books, teachers, ministers—and perhaps your own studies have led to your own theological interpretation of the stories.

You might even be able to write a paper on this chapter and explain it from your theological learning. But theology alone can be cold . . . formal . . . pharisaical. Theology can leave onion-skin pages with underlinings and highlights, but without life, without relevance, without relationship.

What does it mean to "meditate" on the Word of God? Let's try something. Let's center in on these three things and see what we come up with.

The little lamb. We don't know what he was doing, but it certainly wasn't important to him to stay near the shepherd. Did he run off? Did he wander away? Whatever the case, he undoubtedly was driven by one impulse: to take care of his own needs, *his way* . . . finding the grassiest knoll, the most tender shoots, the coolest brook—all by himself—until he's good and *lost*. And all the while the shepherd pursues. He stops and listens. He calls. Can you see him shake his head? *What a foolish lamb. It seems he's just got to rebel. Independent little creature! Trying to run his life his way, do things his way, lead himself to the greenest pastures. How many times is it now that I've found him, barely hanging on?*

But the sheep stubbornly refuses to wait, or turn, or run to his master—unless something happens that he realizes just might be his undoing. He may be bloody, broken, bruised, hungry, hurting, dirty, or smelly, but when the shepherd finds him, he will pick him up and tenderly carry him home.

Can you "play sheep" and feel the warmth of the Shepherd's cloak around you? Can you relax and let Him carry you? Would you like to nestle your head down in the crook of His arm? Do you want to tell Him how sorry you are that you cause Him such distress? Would you like to thank Him for His patience with you? (Draw a picture in your mind of that. Put yourself in the place of the sheep and of the shepherd. What thoughts come to you?)

\* \* \*

The coin doesn't wander or run away. It's just well-hidden. It's deep in a dark crack. It's in a far corner. In an inaccessible place.

But to the owner, that coin is so precious that she *gives herself over* to searching for it diligently and tirelessly, with the anticipation of finding it and securing it once again with her other valuables. It is of great importance to her.

The coin, on the other hand, has no idea of its lost condition. It doesn't feel or think. It just doesn't care, and it doesn't realize how much the woman cares. (Draw a picture of the search in your mind. Put yourself in her place. She's so anxious that the coin be found—salvaged. What does the scene look like from where you're sitting?)

* * *

The son has a free will and the ability to reason. He also has the ability to hurt those who love him. Unlike the shepherd and his sheep or the widow and her coin, the father doesn't search for his son. He just keeps a vigil—a lonely vigil—waiting for the son to decide to come home. Don't you suppose the father would have gone to his son at a moment's notice if he had cried out for help? He was listening. Alert to every sound. If the old dog started barking, he stepped to the door and cocked his head. *He's got to be coming . . . old Rover can smell him!* The slightest sound in the darkest night caused him to quit breathing and strain his ears to listen. *What was that? Is he home?* Just like the shepherd listened for the feeble cry of His lost lamb. And no matter how dirty or smelly or bloody and bruised the boy was, the father would have held him tenderly and carried him home.

The son was certainly as precious as the coin, but the finding-and-taking routine won't work for a son with a mind and will of his own. True, the father would have gone to any inaccessible place to find him, to reach him. Oh, the grief . . . the lost hours that could have been filled with camaraderie, with shared dreams and goals. But a love such as this must sometimes wait. . . . (Can you see it? Feel it. Don't let the black-and-white words camouflage the emotions that are threaded through the days, the hours, the weeks and months of separation. Are you waiting for someone's love? *Is Someone waiting for yours?*)

* * *

This is what it means to meditate on the Word of God, allowing your imagination to put flesh and blood, bone and thought between the rows of black print on white paper. This is how we come to know Him. This is how we come to understand the depth of our Father's love for us.

*Lord, as we study Your Word, please help us to see real people, real pain, real joy . . . and the real You.*

# 20

## *The Bedrock*

*O God, my heart is quiet and confident.*
*No wonder I can sing Your praises!*
*Rouse yourself, my soul!*
*Arise, O harp and lyre!*
*Let us greet the dawn with song!*

*I will thank You publicly throughout the land.*
*I will sing Your praises among the nations.*
*Your kindness and love are as vast as the*
*    heavens.*
*Your faithfulness is higher than the skies.*
*Yes, be exalted, O God, above the heavens.*
*May your glory shine throughout the earth.*

PSALM 57:7–11 TLB

It was probably about this time twenty years ago. . . .

We were in the process of building a house, and please notice that I didn't say "having a house built"! *We* were building this house—the Gillham brood: Bill, Pres, Will, Wade, and Anabel.

I would be ready to "go out to the lot" every morning when the men in the family went their separate ways, and I would work there all day by myself. No fear involved. Just quietness and the sound of my hammer and my slightly off-key, tremolo voice singing songs of praise.

Sometimes I would tack a verse up on a tree or a wall and memorize while I was playing carpenter. How well I remember the morning I was working on Psalm 57:7–11. I had written the verse on a yellow sheet of paper with purple ink and had tacked it on the center brace in the living area. Every time I needed to check and see what came next, I would go by the post.

That's a pleasant memory for me.

I was enjoying the quietness and the solitude of the woods. I was pleased with our progress on the massive project that we had undertaken, and we were growing closer as a family. Sawing. Hammering. Clearing the lot. Planning. Standing back and looking at our handiwork. Getting dirty and sweaty and having picnic lunches. Comparing muscles that were puffing up from hauling the heavy pinta-treated pecan boards. Finding all sorts of surprises, like little snakes and BIG snakes. Spiders and toad frogs. Learning the different trees. Listening to the songs that the birds shared with us. Oh, it was a good time.

My world was turning much slower then.

My stress level was much lower then.

Things are different now, but "my heart is still quiet and confident within me."

*What does that mean, Anabel? How can you separate your heart from the thoughts that shock you* and flit back and forth across your mind? How can you separate your heart from the throbbing, undulating emotions that force you onto this giant rollercoaster ride? How can you separate your heart from your inconsistent, inconsiderate, sometimes downright mean actions?

Well, when all else is peeled away like the layers on an onion—every layer of doubt and confusion, every layer of flesh, every layer of emotions, disappointments, hurt, resentment, discontent, loneliness, and despondency—there is a *bedrock* there. That bedrock, that solid foundation, says, "My commitment to You, dear Lord, is unaltered. There is a confidence, a quietness, a steadfastness."

* * *

*This deepest part of my being becomes so evi- ·*
*dent to me when I'm alone with You, Lord, especially*
*as I was that day at the lot so many years ago—out*
*in Your world of solitude and quietness. So I'm still*
*singing. (He likes to hear me sing.)*
*I still give thanks.*
*I still praise. Why?*
*Not because of my circumstances, but because*
*"Your kindness and Your love are as vast as the heavens.*
*Your faithfulness is higher than the skies."*
*My stress level and my circumstances,*
*where I am and what I'm doing,*
*do not change You, Lord.*
*Please, don't let them change me.*

# 21

## Seeing Jesus

"Don't bother to tell me about your Christ. I know Him. I've seen Him. You've shown Him to me.

"He is a Christ who lingers in the church building on Sunday long after the lights are turned out and everyone has gone home or to the pizza parlor.

"He is a Christ who lives in the quiet sanctuary with all the walnut beams and paneling and sculptured posts.

"He appears in stained glass.

"He makes people laugh and shout and throw up their hands and dance—but just on Sundays.

"A Christ who is buried somewhere in all the lighted candles.

"A Christ who attends funerals and hovers around hospital rooms.

"A Christ who brings tears to the eye when a certain song is sung.

"A Christ who has limits.

"That Christ has no power.

"That Christ is impotent.

"That Christ is not offensive—I just don't need Him. He's not relevant to my life."

*O Lord Jesus. If they really knew You. . . . Relevant to my life? You are my life. You aren't hiding in a building down on Main Street. You haven't unpacked Your suitcase at the hospital. You aren't waiting anxiously for the next funeral to come along so You can "mix and mingle."*

*How we misrepresent You with our hateful tongues and gossip. With our foul language and suggestive remarks. With our depression and constant complaining. With our relentless drive for "things" and with our ruthless ambitions. Small wonder that You seem unnecessary to those whose only witness is a polished, prosperous, and disease-free TV "evangelist." To those whose only glimpse of You is the next-door neighbor who yells at his kids on Sunday morning to "Get in the car, now! Or we'll be late for church!"*

"Me, need Christ?" they ask. "If He's what you have, why should I need Him?"

Oh, that they might know *my* Christ. The life-changing Christ. The Christ who takes the ugly things from my life and gives me understanding for the unlovely, unloving ugly people who wander in and out of my world. Christ, the rebuilder of broken dreams. Christ, the restorer of hope. The Christ who invades my thought-life and keeps it pure. The Christ who never leaves my side but goes with me into every battle, every day. The Christ who holds me and comforts me when I hurt. The Christ who laughs with me and cries with me. Who talks with me and walks with me. Christ, my

Friend. Christ, my Companion. The Christ who watches over me while I sleep, who holds every tear, who hears every sigh. The Christ who loves me more than I can comprehend. The Christ who *died* for me.

*If you would know my Christ,*
*then you would see Jesus.*

# 22

## *Please Love Me*

*Dear Friends,*

**since God loved us as much as that,
we surely ought to love each other too.
For though we have never yet seen God,
when we love each other God lives in us
and His love within us grows ever
stronger.**

**1 JOHN 4:11,12** TLB

My Dear Sister,
     I love you.
Don't ask me why—or how—because I don't understand.
Being human, I've always preferred a certain type in look
     and personality.
Some I'd feel quite comfortable with, and others I would
     avoid.
You are all so very different.
And I don't even know your personality types.
Yet there is this love. Please believe me.

It's Something within me so strong that it causes me to
      reach out and touch you and say, "I love you."
      Please love me.
Not because of my looks or personality, because I know
    you must have your preferences, too.
And I may not meet your qualifications.
Don't expect great things of me—I'm prone to stumble
    and even fall.
And please don't expect me to perform perfectly. I would
    disappoint you.
If your love for me depends on my performance, I'm
    afraid you won't love me for very long.
All I ask is that you accept me as I accept you.
I won't ask you, "How could you really love me?"
Don't ask me, "How could you love so many and know so
    little about them?"

I'll just believe that there is this same Something within
you that causes
      you to reach out to me
      and say,
      "My Dear Sister. I love you, too."

# 23

## Simple, But Maybe Not Easy

**Whatever is born of God overcomes the world; and this is the victory that has overcome the world—our faith.**

1 JOHN 5:4

You may be thinking, *Anabel, the answers that you give—the thoughts that you have—seem almost too simple. Over and over again you talk about Christ living in me, how I am living in Christ, how I must be aware of what's going on in my thought-life.*

*Are you saying that any problem I have, or any problem that anyone else has, can be met through Jesus Christ by incorporating these very simple truths?*

Yes. That's exactly what I'm saying. *Any* problem can be answered through Jesus Christ. If that is *not* true, then His death was in vain for all of us.

Of course, every problem is unique, and there are always practical steps that must be taken when dealing with a problem. But if *you* try to deal with it, to handle these practical steps by yourself instead of allowing

Christ to do it for you, you're heading for frustration and disappointment. Not that everything will work out the way you want it to work out, but He *will* do it all for you.

Who would you rather be in control?
You or Him?

And remember, you are living in Him. What does that mean for you? That the circumstances you are in *will not destroy you;* that you are more than a conqueror, are totally accepted, loved beyond your ability to comprehend, and all of the other beautiful "in Christ" verses.

As to your thought-life: Remember that the Deceiver can defeat you in one way—only one. And that is through your thinking processes. That's why you need to be so alert to the thoughts that play around in your mind.

Perhaps the key word is *control*. God does not force us to walk with Him, for Him, or in obedience to Him. We can walk in rebellion and turn our backs on Him, grieving Him deeply. I am not a robot; neither is my husband, nor are my sons or any of the people in my life who might be the source of pain. I am a human being with the power to choose what I will set my mind on. It is, of course, a matter of accepting or rejecting thoughts.

*It is not what comes into my life that makes or breaks me, but how I handle what comes into my life.*

# 24

## Under His Wings

**The salvation of the righteous is from the Lord; He is their strength in time of trouble. And the Lord helps them, and delivers them; He delivers them from the wicked, and saves them, Because they take refuge in Him.**

PSALM 37:39,40

If I want
> His salvation
> His strength in time of trouble
> His help
> His deliverance, then

I must take refuge *in Him*. These things are found nowhere else but "under His wings"—in His presence.

*Lord, I've never been surrounded by soft wings; I really don't know how that would feel. Maybe like your daddy's lap, or snuggling under the covers when it's awfully cold in the bedroom, or like a feather bed, or sitting in a dark car looking out at a rainstorm that has stopped the traffic.*

*I can imagine it, though . . . the warmth, the softness, the feeling of safety and security. Why, oh why, do I rush around outside in the angry elements, afraid and struggling, depending on my strength and my wisdom to protect me and mine? I remember You cried one time because people refused to come nestle, to let You take care of them.** *

> *Lord, lift Your wings . . .*
> *I'm crawling under.*

* Luke 19:41,42

# 25

## *Lions, Bears, and Giants*

> **The Lord who delivered me from the paw**
> **of the lion and from the paw of the bear,**
> **He will deliver me from the hand of this**
> **Philistine.**
>
> 1 SAMUEL **17:37**

"Hey, you guys. Don't be afraid. I'll fight this Philistine giant."

But David was young. David was not even a warrior, and certainly not an *experienced* warrior. Saul felt it necessary to mention these things after David had so fearlessly declared that he himself would fight Goliath.

But David persisted. "When I am taking care of my father's sheep, and a lion or a bear comes and grabs a lamb from the flock, I go after it with a club and take the lamb from its mouth. If it turns on me I catch it by the jaw and club it to death" (1 Samuel 17:34,35 TLB).

> *If David had not experienced lions and bears,*
> *he would not have been prepared for*
> *his confrontation with Goliath.*

David spent many quiet, lonely hours perfecting his slingshot techniques, figuring out just what size and shape of stone went to the mark most accurately, how far away he could be from his target and still hit it dead center.

*If he hadn't spent those quiet,*
*lonely hours practicing with his slingshot,*
*learning all of those "insignificant" things,*
*would he have been ready to meet the giant?*

David was by himself. He didn't have the company and the encouragement of others.

*But if he had not learned to stand alone,*
*how would he have handled the rejection*
*from Saul and from the people in his kingdom?*

David saw the heart of God and came to know the love of God as he watched over his flocks, leading them, caring for them when they were hurt, agonizing over one little lost lamb.

*The day-by-day routine brought him*
*to an ever-deeper understanding of*
*God's love and of God's ways.*

David met and killed the giant that ridiculed his God and terrorized his nation.

*And as he watched the round stone find its mark,*
*and felt the earth shake when Goliath fell,*
*it was etched indelibly on David's mind and heart*
*that his God was able.*

\* \* \*

*I see all of this, Lord. You were deliberately train-*
*ing David for what You knew would come. Strange. I*
*can see this in the life of David, and yet I always strug-*
*gle with the things that come into my life. What's that*
*old proverb about hindsight?*

*The "things" seem so insignificant at times, Lord,*
*so commonplace, so useless. Are You training me? Will*
*I ever be able to see that my encounters with the "bears*
*and lions" were training sessions? That because of*
*them I was more equipped to meet the "giant" that You*
*knew would appear on my horizon?*

*That's what you call a rhetorical question, isn't it?*
*A question that doesn't need an answer. I know that as*
*I jump over the one-foot hurdle, in the process I'm*
*preparing for the two-foot hurdle. I guess I want the*
*thrill of seeing the giant fall and feeling the ground*
*shake beneath my tired feet. . . .*

*No problem, Lord. I'm not planning on going*
*AWOL. I'm not going to resign from the training pro-*
*gram. (You wouldn't let me, would You?) I know that*
*eventually I'll be a pole-vaulter—of Olympic class. I*
*know that bears and lions lead to giants, and that by*
*Your strength . . . giants fall.*

# 26

## A Message for the Master

**His disciples came and took away
the body and buried it; and they
went and reported to Jesus.**

MATTHEW 14:12

Every time I read it I picture how it must have been . . .

*It was on a cold and windy day
  when they told Him.
Cloaks were wrapped tightly,
  their wet hoods feeble protection
against the cutting rain.
  They walked slowly, wordlessly
along the road . . . the rain nourishing
  the freshly planted seeds of confusion.
Some wept, I'm sure. Others
  retreated—broken—into the tired
and lonely corners of their minds.*

*They found Him in the Garden.
  He wasn't praying—just standing,
as a father might stand just before
  receiving news of a son lost in battle.*

*All of eternity stood between the silent stares*
*that lurked in the hooded caves.*
*A large man with a hoarse voice*
*interrupted the rain's one-way conversation*
*with the earth:*

*"Master . . . they have beheaded John."*

W.M.G.

# 27

## Knowing Where the Rabbits Are

The magician was truly awesome! He held the audience in the palm of his hand from the moment the house-lights dimmed, playing with their emotions as deftly as a gifted musician.

"Where did those rabbits come from?"
"How did those scarves get in there?"
"That saw *has* to be cutting into that woman! Look where it is!"
"I can't watch!"

His *acts* left them bordering on hysteria—enormously impressed, greatly amazed, completely bewildered.

But while the crowd gasped with disbelief, his assistant watched—*unperturbed*. And when the time was right, she played her part as she had been taught. She had seen the acts many times before; but more than that, she knew how the magician worked. She watched with great calm as the woman was "sawn in two." She counted the rabbits to be sure none of them wriggled to freedom, and she carefully folded the scarves into their hidden compartments. The acts were impressive, but she knew the magician's *ways*.

*He made known His ways to Moses,*
*His acts to the sons of Israel.*

*What's wrong with my plan, God? It seems to me
like a good way to solve the problem. But do something,
won't You? Time's getting away from us. What good
could possibly come from this? Why did You allow this
to come into my life in the first place? Are You listening
to me, Lord? I've been talking to You about this for a
long, long time. Making this come out right would be
such a little thing for You to do. Why do You let this continue in my life? Don't You think it's about time to call
this situation to a screeching halt? Lord, why?*

What I'm saying is, "I don't understand what You're
doing! I don't understand Your *ways.*"

*That's why the children of Israel were always so
discontent, isn't it, Lord? Your acts were the sole proof
to them that You were still around, and so they mur-
mured between acts, having no idea of the amazing
preparations that were being carried out during the in-
termission.*

*Lord, I want to know Your ways. I don't want to be
confused and ignorant of Your plans, controlled by fear
or frustration, by pain or emotional distress. I want to
watch—unperturbed—Your acts, carrying out my as-
signments as I have been taught—confident—helping*

*You prepare during the intermissions, and all the while understanding Your ways. And Lord, I don't want to change them—I really don't.*

*I just want to assist You in Your very impressive program.*

# 28

## Love That Never Lets You Go

**Apart from Me you can do nothing.**

**JOHN 15:5**

Can you imagine God, scowling and with His finger pointing straight at you, saying . . .

"Look, I have led you this far—but NO FURTHER!

You're on your own from here on out. I have to eventually cut the apron strings, don't I? You have to learn to walk by yourself.

For too long now you have depended on Me. It will cripple you to have Me constantly supplying and supporting you, continually advising and interpreting for you, strengthening you by My constant presence.

I created you to stand on your own two feet. I gave you intelligence. I gave you a will. When are you going to learn to take it on the chin? When are you going to learn to take care of your problems by yourself? Now rest assured, I'll be in the shadows watching, but you are now in control. And don't yell for Me the first time you stump your toe, either. You can do it! Hear Me? You can do it!"

*Read that again*. How does it affect you?

Of course it's not true. And yet, as I read it my emotions start up, my stomach starts around, and my body wants to sit down.

*Would you believe that this was the way I faced life for years?*

Maybe you're sitting in the same row where I sat. This is man's idea of God—the God he would "build." His conjecture. This is man and his interpretation of God and the role He plays in our lives.

If this were God, I would have long ago resigned from the choir and abandoned my Sunday school class to search for a God who was interested in *me*. To hunt for a God who *cared*. To seek a God who was powerful enough to heal my wounds, to pick me up, to be my strength. And I would not give up until I found Him. . . .

> *Come to me, all of you who are weary and over-burdened, and I will give you rest! Put on my yoke and learn from me. For I am gentle and humble in heart and you will find rest for your souls. For my yoke is easy and my burden is light.*
>
> MATTHEW **11:28,29** PHILLIPS

There is a God like this. His name is Jesus.

*"You will seek Me and find Me when you search for Me with all your heart. And I will be found by you," declares the Lord.*

JEREMIAH **29:13,14**

I rush to find Him.
I need Him desperately.
I want to know Him.
I love Him.

# 29

## Casting Your Burdens on Him

*He's hurting again, Lord, and there's nothing I can do about it. It's been such a long ordeal. How much can he endure?*

*She moved out . . . she's gone . . . what did I say? What did I do? God, I tried so hard to be the mother she needed me to be.*

*How long is this going to go on? I don't think I can endure the loneliness another single day.*

**Cast your burden upon the Lord, and He will sustain you.**

**PSALM 55:22**

**Casting all your anxiety upon Him, because He cares for you.**

**I PETER 5:7**

What do you do with *your* burdens? People and circumstances that seem to drain every ounce of your strength, things you would like to give to the Lord but just can't seem to let go of?

God showed me how to give my burdens to Him . . . a simple little exercise, but oh so wonderful to experience. I'd like to share it with you.

You'll need about 30 minutes alone. Gather a few things together from home: an envelope, a piece of paper, a pen, a watch (preferably with a second hand), and a felt-tipped pen. Go buy a helium-filled balloon. Then immediately go somewhere where there are no obstacles, no trees or buildings—maybe a deserted football stadium or a park or a lake.

Take all your paraphernalia with you to the edge of the water or the center of the field. Write about your burden on the balloon with your felt-tipped pen, anything that will help you associate that balloon with your problem. Find a rock about the size of a half-brick, and hold it and the string to your balloon in your hand, lifting it with a straight arm at a 45-degree angle. Heavy, isn't it?

Begin talking to the Lord about your burden—all your thoughts, your fears, the pain, the destroyed dreams. As you are praying, your arm is going to get awfully tired. *Keep right on praying.* Tell Him *everything*. Any of the thoughts that you have had—vomit it all out—if there is bitterness, anger, depression—all of it.

By now you're crying, and you can't separate the emotional pain from the physical pain you're experiencing because your arm is hurting so badly. Then, *when you cannot hold your arm up another single second*, say something like this: "Lord, You have commanded me to give my burdens to You. I can't handle this. It's too much for me. I can't hold onto it any longer. You must take it."

*Drop the rock, release the string, and watch that burden float up into the heavens—into the open, waiting arms of God.*

Thank Him for telling you to give Him your burden—and for taking it. Look at your watch and record the time and date on your piece of paper. Write this: *On (date/time), I gave my burden to the Lord. And He took it.* (Print that last line.)

Look up into the sky and find that tiny speck. *It's His*—it is no longer yours. It's not in your hand. He told you to give it to Him, and you did. Now fold your paper and put it in your envelope (where is the balloon? catch one last glimpse of it). Seal it, and on the outside write "GOD" and then the date.

When you get home, get an index card and cut it into strips. On each strip write just the date. Put a strip over the sink, one in your bathroom medicine cabinet by your toothbrush, one on the dash of your car—anyplace where you can glance at it—and thank Him for taking your burden. (Close your eyes and visualize that speck in the sky again.)

Please know that I love you. I understand. Oh, not completely, but I long to help. I pray that this simple exercise will give you peace. Remember, your emotions are not the barometer of peace. KNOWING that He has taken your burden and will handle it with wisdom and loving tenderness is the key to peace. (Remember how that balloon went straight to Him when you released it?) *Think on these things.*

*Just as my child brings his broken toys*
*with tears*
*for me to mend,*
*I took my broken dreams to God*
*because He was my Friend.*
*But then . . . instead of leaving Him*
*in peace*
*to work alone,*
*I hung around and tried to help*
*with ways that were my own.*
*At last I snatched them back*
*and cried,*
*"How could You be so slow?"*
*"What could I do, My child?" He said.*
*"You never did let go."*

Faith Mitchner

# 30

## Trusting Him with My Burdens

God has told me to give Him my burdens, remember?

**_Cast your burden upon the Lord, and He will sustain you._**

**PSALM 55:22**

I sincerely want to do this. I know He is much more capable than I am when it comes to handling life's problems. He's always present on the scene, able to choreograph circumstances to the best interest of the person for whom I am concerned. I _know_ these things, but do I _really_ trust Him to handle the burdens I give Him?

\* \* \*

I had several sacks to give to the Salvation Army, so I called to ask them to come by, then placed the sacks on the front porch so they could pick them up whether I was home or not.

Thursday was pickup day. But I got my days mixed up and thought they were to come on Wednesday, and when they didn't show up I thought that they had forgotten me and my sacks. I'd go to the door . . . yep! sacks still there. It's raining. Go out and move the sacks. Night came. Will the sacks be safe? Then on Thursday they were late in coming, and so once again I assumed the responsibility for "watching over the sacks." Then they came! I watched them drive away with *my* sacks in their truck; they had *changed hands* and were not my *burden* any longer.

Now I didn't call them a single time to check on those sacks. I trusted them to handle the things I gave them to the best of their ability, and, since they do this kind of work all the time, to do their job well.

> The question:
> Have I done as much with the burden I have given to the Lord?

> Is He capable?
> Has it really been "picked up"?
> What if it rains?
> What will happen when night comes?
> Do I trust Him as much as I trusted those men who picked up my sacks?

*Oh, I do, Lord, I do! You came at my request. You picked up my burden, put it in Your truck, and drove off. Now I must trust You to work with what I gave to You; and since You do this kind of work all the time, I'm sure You will do it well.*

> An afterthought:
>> Leave it to the Lord to use sacks of unwanted and outgrown clothing to remind me of just what it means to throw my burdens on Him.

# 31

## A Very Present Help

*There is that intense need again, Lord.*

*I don't really know why it comes or where it comes from.*

*It's that need to be alone—to isolate myself. But I know that's an impossibility. My world revolves around the "others" in it.*

*The press of people, the demand of duties, the tyranny of the urgent—they have all dealt hard blows to my chosen path of quiet contentment and joyous victory.*

*Of course, I know that You can and will overcome this sense of being pushed and pulled and shoved and put on display. How many times have I experienced Your tenacious devotion when this happens to me? Your power. Your wisdom. Your love. Your patience.*

*I guess my feeling of weariness and weakness only enables You to move more freely.*

*Thank You, Lord, for rescuing me—for pulling me out of the depths. I know that I could NOT face life without You—indeed, I would choose to not face life without You.*

*But then, how could I separate You from me?*
*You ARE—me.*
*I am—You.*

*You are my Source of Life—the breath I*
*breathe.*
*You are my Motivator in Life—my reason*
*for breathing.*
*You are my Goal in Life—my prize—the*
*finish line.*

❀ ❀ ❀

*In Him we live and move and exist.*

*God, in whose hand are your life-breath*
*and your ways.*

*In whose hand is the life of every living thing*
*and the breath of all mankind.*

ACTS 17:28
DANIEL 5:23
JOB 12:10

# 32

## A Worm with Wings

The yard is one of my "therapy clinics." (What *do* you think about when you're digging holes for the jasmine shoots or pulling up weeds?) I always wind up with dirt caked on my hands and knees, and with a respectable amount on my face and in my hair. The dirtier I get, the more fun it is! (Small wonder the boys loved to play in the dirt, and still are drawn to the messy stuff!)

I was undergoing my "yard therapy" one day, but it was being interrupted. Someone somewhere was unhappy and was being very verbal about it. Whoever it was, his grumpy whining was ruining my hour of much-needed solitude.

Investigation and confrontation were in order, so I followed the disagreeable sounds until I spotted the culprit. *It was a butterfly*—talking to himself! I stood there listening to him rant and rave. He was lamenting his woeful, miserable condition.

*Oh, how I hate crawling along this limb, eating this horrible elm leaf. Worm food! How I would love to soar with the wind, but here I am, stuck in a tree. Look at those beautiful flowers. If only I could taste the nectar. The life of a worm is not a happy one . . . depressing and confining. But then, God made some vessels for common use, and I guess that's me—common.*

I walked over, stood very close to that disillusioned little butterfly, and said to him, "You silly thing, acting for all the world like you're a worm—eating worm food and wishing you could take the wind to any flower your heart desired. And you believe that this is your God-given fate! Have you never realized you have *wings?* That all you have to do is spread them? Don't you know who you are? You are a *butterfly!*"

Like the butterfly
I find
I can no longer stay behind
the self-made walls
of my own apprehensive fears,
behind the crust of my old cocoon.
Because of Him I am free
to break through the walls that once were me
and to soar into
God's dimension

*Oh, by the way, from one butterfly to another: Would you like to go flying with me this afternoon?*

# 33

## *Refreshment in the Desert*

*How blessed is the man whose strength is in Thee,*
   *In whose heart are the highways to Zion!*
*Passing through the valley of Baca, they make it a*
*spring;*
   *The early rain also covers it with blessings.*
*They go from strength to strength.*

PSALM 84:5–7

*How blessed is the man whose strength is*
*in You . . .*

Do I seek blessings? Of course.
Am I always sure of the route to take to receive
a blessing? No.
Well, here is a route that is guaranteed.
*The man who has come to know that You are his*
*strength is a man who is blessed.*

If I have come to know that *You* are my strength,
then in all probability I've been drawing strength from
some other source—myself, no doubt—and this "other"
strength has disappointed me. It hasn't worked. It hasn't

been effective. Perhaps I've tried many avenues seeking to rejuvenate that strength, and, after humiliating failures, frustration, emotional pain, and step-by-sometimes-painful step, I have come to the conclusion that I don't have the strength.

For me this has been a process whereby I have come to know something that I didn't know before. I have arrived at a point of truth and realization: *My strength is in You.* Therefore I am blessed.

That leaves no room for doubt, for hesitancy, for argument. The question is, *If I have come to* know *that God is my strength, why am I not* always *blessed?* The answer: Because I do not always walk in what I have come to *know!*

### *In whose heart are the highways to Zion . . .*

Said another way: In whose heart there is a deep desire to walk in Your will.

As the new creature in Christ Jesus that I am, it *is* my deep desire to walk in Your will. I now have "the laws of God written on my heart," and I "joyfully concur with the law of God in the inner man," so this requirement has been met. It was met by You at the cross.

And once again, the man whose deep desire is to walk in Your will is a man who is blessed—*unequivocally.* This blessing is mine as I commit myself to walk in Your will, trusting in Your strength. And this doesn't mean I will always "perform" perfectly. That isn't what it says. It has to do with my heart's desire.

*Passing through the valley of Baca, they make it a spring . . .*

The valley of Baca, a *desert*. This Scripture doesn't identify what the difficulties of the "desert" may be, or how intense, how painful, how lengthy, how wrought with frustration—just difficult circumstances that plunge into my life. I would say that anything, small or large, that I find difficult to handle would qualify, from a small irritation to a devastating, tragic event.

*These very difficulties become a source—a spring.* But a spring reached only through hardships. This indicates another "process": Difficulties were not always this way for me, but they have *become* a source. A change takes place. I take another route. I view the difficult times that come into my life *differently*.

*A source.* A source of heat is a fire. A source of light is the sun. A source of vegetables is a garden—a source is where something originates. It's hard for me to see "difficulties" as the source where refreshment is going to be found. But I have experienced it, so I bypass the logical deduction and go with what I have come to *know* as Truth: *With Your strength as my strength, desiring Your will in my heart, the desert of hardship becomes for me a spring.*

I picture a person gulping water, either on all fours by a riverbed or drinking from a large glass with water spilling over the edges onto his coat—no thought of cost, of whose property the stream is on, of wet clothing—just satisfying the deep thirst.

What happens to a man who drinks deeply from a spring? He is strengthened, refreshed. . . the water ministers to his whole system. And I must keep in mind that the spring is *God's* power, not mine.

Is this power—this source—capable of meeting my problems? I would be hesitant to answer *if I had not experienced this myself*. For example: I have never *experienced* flying in a helicopter, so I can't discuss that with you. I can tell you how I *think* it might be, based on what I've heard from other people, but I don't know for sure. To *experience* something means I can speak with some authority on that subject: I know what it is like because I have been there. Well, I *have* drunk from His cool water when I've been so very tired and thirsty, and I know what happens. I *have* experienced it. And I assure you, it meets every test.

### *The early rain also covers it with blessings . . .*

I can't think of anything that would communicate more beautifully just how blessed the man is whose strength is in You and whose heart desires Your will than the descriptive phrase "invigorating, early spring rain." Everything about it is so clean, so fresh, so alive. The air is sweet. The birds are singing. The drops of water sparkle on the flowers and trees, and the sky is startlingly blue. I want to take a deep breath and throw back my shoulders, facing with new strength my world. I am refreshed. I am blessed. You have touched my life.

***They go from strength to strength . . .***

*I do not have to be strong.* I tap into *His* strength.
Is His strength sufficient? What a ridiculous question!
And yet, how often do I, through my behavior, express
doubt as to the sufficiency of His strength? I can't "run
out" of His strength. When I've exhausted one supply,
there's another ready and waiting—it's never-ending. I
go from strength to strength.

> *O Lord, I thank You that the difficulties that
> come into my life today can be a source of
> refreshment and peace and joy for me. And
> how I thank You for my new heart and for
> the strength that You have given me for
> meeting every second of this new day.*

# 34

## A Friend of Jesus

"Lazarus!"

The eight-year-old boy was on his hands and knees in the garden, pulling the weeds from around the tender green plants, when he heard the familiar voice.

*That's Jesus! I didn't know they were coming for a visit.*

"Mom! Mary and Joseph and Jesus are here!" The two boys had been friends a long time . . . *best friends*. They enjoyed being together, especially each year when they would all go to Jerusalem for the Feast of the Passover. And then there were the special times—rare, of course—but times like today, when the hours would fly as they grabbed for the seconds and filled every minute.

*It's so much fun when Jesus comes. I have such a good time.*

❋ ❋ ❋

"Lazarus!"

"Hey! Over here, Jesus!"

"Ask your mother if you can come walk with us so I can tell you about what happened in the Temple today."

"Is that where they found You? Your folks have been frantic . . . looking for You everywhere."

"I'm sorry about worrying them. But it's all so strange, Lazarus. Can I talk to you about it?"

The two walked along, arms interlocked, growing ever closer as they grew older and shared the secrets of their young lives. Lazarus knew his Friend was someone very special.

&#42; &#42; &#42;

"Lazarus!"

"That's Jesus, Martha. How good to hear Him. Prepare a special meal for us and we'll all visit together. By the way, where's Mary? Get her to help you.

"I'm back here, Jesus. Oh, I've *missed* seeing You. Let's go to the roof where it's cool and You can tell me what's been happening. I've been hearing some wonderful reports about Your ministry. And I hear there's some solid opposition, too. I've been anxious to talk with You."

"It's good to be with you, Lazarus. Let me go in and say hello to Martha and Mary before we go upstairs."

&#42; &#42; &#42;

"Lazarus!"

"Mary! Martha! Come quickly! Jesus is here."

"Hello, dear friend. I'm on my way to Jerusalem and needed to be with you this evening. Can you find room for me?"

"Oh, Jesus, You know You are always welcome in our home. We look forward to Your being here, and I miss you very much. We've been friends a long time. There's no one I feel closer to or that I would rather be with than You. You're very important in my life."

\* \* \*

"Lazarus!"

"Lazarus! Come forth!"

Lazarus tried to open his eyes . . . just to think about moving seemed to be an effort. It was as though his arms were bound . . . as though his legs were wrapped. The smell. The dampness. The darkness. And it's cold.

*Jesus? Are You calling me? Where am I? This is like . . . almost like a tomb.*

"Lazarus!"

*It is Jesus. But He sounds so far away.*

Slowly he got to his feet, struggling at the tightly wound burial cloths, remembering vaguely the illness and the last touch from his beloved sisters, groping toward the light that filtered dimly into the blackness.

*I'm coming, Jesus. I hear You, dear Friend. I'm moving kind of slowly, but wait on me . . . I need to talk with You about something that happened to me just last week. . . .*

\* \* \*

What role did Lazarus play in Jesus' life? I know Jesus spent a lot of time in Bethany. He must have enjoyed being there. He felt loved. Comfortable. At home. Did He appreciate a clean bed and a hot meal?

*Oh, I'm so prone to make You into an "untouchable God" instead of a beloved Friend. And I don't need—or really want—an untouchable God. I do need a Friend. Someone whose voice is familiar to me. Someone that I long to be with. Someone who misses me and Someone that I miss. Someone that I can lock arms with and we can walk together and talk about things that are important to us.*

*Lord, I want to be a Lazarus to You.*
*I want to be Your dear friend.*

# 35

## *Free to Serve*

I think I might have reacted the same way Peter did.

*"Lord! You are not about to wash my feet!"*

Peter, they say, was impulsive, and had his foot in his mouth most of the time. I relate to Peter. He was honest. He was open. He didn't try to make people think he understood everything about Jesus, but he wanted to understand. So he said things that were sometimes embarrassing to the others.

*"Lord, You know me inside and out. I don't need just a foot-washing. I need to be washed from my hands to my head! All of me!"*

Yes. I relate to Peter. He knew himself and he knew his Lord: "You are the Christ, the Son of the living God" (Matthew 16:15,16).

To let Jesus, the Son of the living God, get down on His knees and wash my feet would be something I could hardly endure. So humiliating! That's not His place!

As if washing feet or not washing feet determines who you are. No. Washing feet may be what I do to make ends meet here on earth, but it doesn't dictate who I am.

It didn't bother Jesus at all. You see, He knew who He was. He knew that the Father had given all things into His hands. He knew that He had come forth from God and He knew that He was going back to God (John 13:3).

Incredible! Knowing who He was—and *serving*. But then, He said that He didn't come to be served, but to serve. That should make us stop and think and try to put everything together.

He turned right around and did the very same thing again the night of the fish fry (John 21:13). This was after the cross. After the resurrection. He had conquered death. He had proven Himself to be God's Anointed One. He had revealed Himself to His disciples as the Messiah, as the risen Lord, and yet—He built the charcoal fire, He cooked the fish, and then He *served* them.

Not only did *He* know who He was now, but they too knew who He was—without a whisper of a doubt. How uncomfortable they must have been! I can imagine Peter saying, "Lord, please come sit over here and let me take care of that. I'd feel so much better if You'd let me serve You."

Jesus said to them in effect, "You don't understand, do you? I've given you an example. If I, Your Lord, have served you, then you ought to serve each other" (John 13:34). Maybe it seems like a demeaning act to you now, but one of these days You will understand just who you are, and then you too will be free to serve."

❈ ❈ ❈

I too am an heir of God (Romans 8:16,17). I have been given every spiritual blessing in the heavenly places (Ephesians 1:3). God created me and has a plan for my life (Ephesians 2:10). I know that I became a child of God when I was born again (John 1:12,13), and I know that I'm going to be with God (John 14:3). I know my true identity. Birth determines that. I know who I am.

And do you know what that means to me? Why, I can wash feet and make the fire and cook the supper and serve without it bothering me. It sets me free . . . to *serve*.

# 36

## Doing God's Will

*Rejoice always, pray without ceasing, in everything give thanks; for this is God's will for you in Christ Jesus.*

### 1 THESSALONIANS 5:16–18

\* \* \*

I think I'm seeking His will for me as I plan my day—praying about things: just how much I should be involved in the lives of my boys; what phone calls I should make; should I send a note to Nancy; should I accept the chairmanship of that committee; seeking His guidance even in my grocery shopping; yet all the while I'm fretting about some of the things the boys are going through or getting frustrated when the sweeper conks out, resenting the mundane chores that seem never to end—and there's my constant battle with depression.

Then I come face-to-face with 1 Thessalonians 5:16–18. I stop. And I think. Am I walking in His revealed will for me, rejoicing and giving thanks in everything and praying constantly? Am I practicing those things that I *know* are His will—that are not a "nebulous leading" but written, direct instruction?

How illogical I am sometimes! And I was so proud of all of my efforts and my prayers. (*My* efforts and *my* prayers). I had my *own* little conversations going with God about *my* daily routine. (Impressive!) Choosing what I think He *might* want me to do instead of what He has told me to do. But then, "doing" is so much easier (and more visible) than "rejoicing" or "praying" or "thanking." Not doing what I ask is what I would call disobedience or rebellion in *my* child.

Here I am praying, "Lord, show me Your will for my life today." And He's saying, "But Anabel, I have. And you're ignoring it."

\* \* \*

*Lord, I don't want to be disobedient to Your Word, Your instructions, Your law—Your will. I understand that I should be obedient to what I have received before presuming to ask for more. Only You can accomplish this for me—through me.*

*Thank You, dear One.*

# 37

## Going Home

I was pondering death one day, immersed in the loneliness that is inevitable when someone you have loved so very much isn't a part of your life any longer.

I would no longer be going to Poteau "for a few days to be with Mother." I wouldn't be calling to talk to her about the books she was reading or about one of her delicious recipes. I wouldn't be sending the flowers that she loved so dearly. *She was simply no longer there.*

The finality of a lost relationship is beyond comprehension. It only becomes reality as the days pass. Granma Hoyle, Aunt Lucy, Uncle Al—they had all been gone for years. My beloved Dad and dear, sweet, little Mason—and now, Mother.

These thoughts came to me and over the years have become very precious. I would like to share them with you. . . .

\* \* \*

College days. So long ago and far away! But they were good times, and my life was not too awfully complicated then. My family was still "intact," and they loved me. They were proud of me. I was very special to them, and they were very special to me.

I went to Northeastern State College in Tahlequah, Oklahoma. I know—you've never heard of it. That's all right. Of course, I didn't have a car to go back and forth between Tahlequah and Poteau, my beloved hometown, about a three-hour drive away. So I frequented the bus station.

Perhaps you remember how those bus trips were: The driver would dutifully announce, in his best monotone, the towns as we would approach them. (That monotone must have been one of the requirements for being a bus driver!) As he did so, certain people would gather their belongings, stand at the exit, and then get off. They were home. Where they had been or how long they had been gone or the circumstances that brought them back—none of those things concerned me. Just the thrill of going home!

I didn't know any of the people getting off, but as I got closer and closer to Poteau, I'd get more and more excited!

"Westville."

"Stilwell.

"Sallisaw" . . . and I knew I had less than an hour left.

Mother and Daddy would be there to meet me when I stepped off the bus. My anticipation grew because I knew just what to expect. Everything was going to be prepared for me. My room would be spotlessly cleaned, and there would be a single red carnation in a bud vase on my dresser. There would be fried chicken, chocolate pie, fresh tomatoes, and probably an "almost finished" new dress that Mother would have ready for me to try on. All of my favorite things! How dear to remember it even now. And I know that those people who got off at Westville and Stilwell—who were secure in their love from the people they were meeting—felt just like I did.

*There's Cavanaugh mountain!*

"Spiro." (Thirty minutes.)

"Panama." (Fifteen minutes.)

"Shady Point." Almost there . . . *almost home!*

\* \* \*

In my life, I'm "riding the bus" with Mason and Dad, Mom and Pop, Mother and all of my other dear ones. I certainly didn't dream that my little boy, Mace, was going to get up—step off the bus—and be Home that day in May of 1972. Nor that Mother would smile and wave goodbye and step through the door on June 22, 1981. She was Home! And the people who were meeting her! There's Marcus, her beloved husband, Aunt Lucy and Uncle Al, Grandma Cummins, Mace . . . how exciting! How wonderful!

I don't turn around and look at their empty seats and think about things I never said, or things that I did say. I don't linger, remembering how much fun we had as we rode together. I don't think about the experiences we shared through the trip. No, that's a "luxury" that I do not afford myself.

Instead, I think of the clean room with the single red carnation on the dresser . . . the fried chicken . . . the chocolate pie . . . the fresh tomatoes. I think about all the preparations for the gala Homecoming.

And, of course, I don't know who in my circle of love is going to begin gathering their things together and get off at the next stop. But I do know that if I can just see with spiritual eyes, I will see them smile, wave good-bye, and dash into the waiting arms of loved ones—smothered with kisses and held once more in those embraces that had been only a poignant memory for years and years. And ultimately they will be ushered into the waiting arms of our beloved Jesus! Incomparable! More than wonderful!

I'm getting closer and closer as my hair begins to thin and my scalp shows through the gray, as it gets a bit more difficult to get up, once I've gotten down. Maybe the driver is calling out "Stilwell" about now. And the anticipation is building. They'll be watching for me and everything will be ready! They love me. I'm secure in that. And, best of all, Jesus will be there . . . with open arms. Oh! I am beginning to get so excited about finally getting . . . HOME!

❈ ❈ ❈

*May the Lord bless you, dear one, and fill your life with anticipation.*

# 38

## New Beginnings

**His lovingkindness begins afresh each day.**
LAMENTATIONS 3:23 TLB

A new month. Always a challenge. More, it seems, than a new day—but those are a challenge, too.

*I thank You, Lord, for new days, new hours, new minutes, for even the new seconds! New beginnings.*

**Teach us to number our days and recognize how few they are; help us to spend them as we should.**

PSALM 90:12 TLB

*Yesterday—the day before today and the day before that—were bad days, Lord. What makes a bad day? I'd like to say my topsy-turvy world or the people around me or my circumstances, but I know that isn't true. The only way I can have a bad day is by not allowing You to handle the day.*

*The battle is not yours but God's.*

2 CHRONICLES 20:15

Well, on this particular day my view is un-
clouded, and for this I thank You. It's pretty neat
when I open my eyes and can see clearly out my
window. I don't have to fret about things like wear-
ing my oxfords to keep my feet from getting wet; I
don't have to change my hairdo because of what happens when it's "spray versus moisture"; I don't have
to start hunting for my umbrella or turn on my fog
lights or cancel my plans because there's simply no
way to see through the heavy mists.

**I have learned to be content in whatever
circumstances I am.**

PHILIPPIANS 4:11

Yes, I thank You, but I will not—I simply will
not—praise You simply because my horizons are
clear. Tomorrow my horizon may be so cloudy that I
can't see my hand in front of my face! I praise You
for who You are and what You are—not for what You
do. This way I will never question praising You, will
I, Lord (especially when I have another "bad" day)?

**This is the day which the Lord has made;
Let us rejoice and be glad in it.**

PSALM 118:24

*I ask that this new month be a new start for me, allowing You to live through me more completely than I did yesterday or the other yesterdays that made up the month before yesterday.*

*I just* must *remember three basic things:*

> *You are God.*
> *You love me.*
> *You are my life.*

*If I walk in these three truths, my day is successfully finished BEFORE IT HAS EVEN BEGUN. No circumstance, however tragic, can alter these truths, for none of them are controlled by cloudy or clear horizons.*

Maybe Paul won't mind if I paraphrase his final declaration of victory in his second letter to Timothy (4:7) and make it fit my day.

"The glorious fight God gave me I have fought." God gave me today, with all of its events, and I have met each one with *His* strength.

"The course I was set I have finished." He planned a set course for me and I followed the plan. Through everything I have kept thinking about His love, His life, and my responsibility: to let Him love me and to let Him live His life through me, for me.

"And I have kept the faith."

*I just can't go wrong when I do that, can I, Lord?*

# 39

## *Everyday Miracles*

*He who . . . changes deep darkness into morning, who also darkens day into night.*

**AMOS 5:8**

*The dawn and the sunset shout for joy.*

**PSALM 65:8** TLB

*Have you ever watched God make a morning?*

Set your alarm and stumble out into the quiet shadows of an unborn day. Have a chair ready (and some mosquito repellent). Then watch carefully as God "changes deep darkness into morning."

And how long has it been since you observed God "darken day into night"?

Plan an evening with your chair out on the lawn facing west. Marvel at His power, His creative coloring. Remember that He watched it and said, "This is good."

*God made two huge lights, the sun and the moon, to shine down upon the earth—the larger one, the sun, to preside over the day and the smaller one, the moon, to preside through the night; he had also made the stars. And God set them in the sky to light the earth, and to preside over the day and night, and to divide the light from the darkness. And God was pleased.*

GENESIS 1:16–18 TLB

\* \* \*

*Lord, I must confess that there are times when I have complained about not seeing miracles—You know, the lame walking, the blind seeing. And yet there is a ball of fire hanging in the sky, and another hanging ball that reflects the light of the big one, and billions of twinkling ones! What creative genius! Oh, there are burning bushes all around me when I take the time to look. And if I listen carefully, I just might hear a shout or two!*

Earth's crammed with heaven,
And every common bush afire with God;
And only he who sees takes off his shoes—
The rest sit round it and pluck blackberries.

Elizabeth Barrett Browning

# 40

## Promised Suffering, Promised Comfort

*Just as the sufferings of Christ are ours in abundance, so also our comfort is abundant through Christ.*

2 CORINTHIANS 1:5

Here is something very important that we must realize: Christ never allows *abundant sufferings* without providing *abundant comfort.*

*It is so easy for me to accept and expect the abundant comfort that Your Word promises me, Lord, but I find it difficult to accept (and certainly to expect) the abundant sufferings. . . .*

*But then, if I were to practice walking in Your abundant comfort all the time, I wouldn't be caught short when the sufferings start knocking on my door. (Or do they knock? Generally it seems they just open the door and walk in unannounced.)*

*Can I separate one from the other? It seems to me that I won't fully appreciate Your comfort until I've gone through the suffering. The question I must answer is this:*

**Just how important is it to me that I experience Your abundant comfort?**

# 41

## *Grace, Not Deliverance*

We can't deny that painful circumstances invade our lives. But we must put them in their proper perspective.

Pres, my eldest, was going through a time of deep disillusionment, hurt, loneliness, confusion, and penetrating self-evaluation. He shared with me how the following thoughts brought clarity in his thinking, how they enveloped him in peace and promised endurance.

\* \* \*

Pres:

"I know that the difficult circumstances in my life at this present moment are very real. But I also *know* that Christ has provided victory for me *in* these circumstances.

"As you and I well know, this victory is not *deliverance* but *grace,* as spoken of in Proverbs 3:34: 'He gives grace to the afflicted.'

"Grace used here refers to the divine influence upon your heart brought about through the affliction, the difficulties—difficulties such as I am experiencing now, and how that divine influence is reflected in your life through the unexpected benefits of the suffering."

*Unexpected benefits? Like what? What might we learn from suffering? How does it change us, and what can we profit from it?*

It might be . . .

the rebirth of compassion for others

a renewal of your covenant with Christ

an awareness of His amazing strength
through you

the thankfulness and joy that will emanate
from the depths of your inner being

coming to know—really know—how much He
loves you, and responding to that love

the tender knowledge of your complete
acceptability by God, your Maker.

Pres again:

"Deliverance is the easy way out. *Grace is a training ground run through tear-blurred eyes which, in the end, leaves your heart strong, your muscles toned, and your head clear and organized.*"

He has said to me:

**"I am with you; that is all you need. My power shows up best in weak people."**
**2 CORINTHIANS 12:9 TLB**

*Thank You, Lord, for in these—my WEAKEST moments—I will be strong beyond my ability to comprehend.*

**125**

# 42

## *The Witness of Suffering*

David. What a magnetic person he must have been. And the influence of his life goes on and on. He's influenced my life. And yet, the years between us are many and the comparisons few. . . .

David was a powerful king.

> *I'll never be a political figure. One good reason is that I'm too old, but I wouldn't head down that street even if I were young again. I'm too sensitive, and I'm not aggressive enough. I wouldn't mind meeting the baby-kissing requirement, but I have no desire to take on the problems of a nation.*

David was a mighty, fearless warrior.

> *I could never go into a battle or map out strategic battle plans. I have real difficulty with maps. Oh yes, I've been a "self-appointed" and chosen leader most of my life, but I suffer from an incurable disease diagnosed as "basic terror." I'm just not cut out to be a warrior.*

David was a musician.

> *I've always said that God knew exactly what He was doing when He didn't give me a lovely voice or supple fingers that could slide skillfully over the strings of a guitar or master the coordination of trumpet valves. So far, David and I don't have a great deal in common.*

David wrote lyrics for his music. He was a poet.

> *I can write jingles and quickies and the occasional poem with deep thoughts and unusual meter, but that too is an area where my skill falls far short of David's.*

David was a man who suffered greatly.

> *Well, we've finally found some common ground, something that happens in my world. I'm very well acquainted with suffering, with troubles and pain. (Are you?)*

There's only one thing that opens the door for me to say, "David, I relate to you." The mighty kingdom and the noteworthy battles are all history—ancient history. The kingdom toppled and the battles had to be fought again. And no doubt David is singing his songs and playing a harp now, but I'll probably be an expert musician, too, when I get to Heaven. I'll challenge him for first chair in the orchestra!

But none of those things matter. David did one thing that immortalized him: David kept a record of his suffering—he wrote many of the Psalms. How many millions of people have read his words, immersed in similar anxieties and pain, and gathered strength to face their world?

*The Lord is my Shepherd, I shall not want.*
PSALM 23:1

*When my anxious thoughts multiply within me, Thy consolations delight my soul.*
PSALM 94:19

*It is God who arms me with strength and makes my way perfect.*
PSALM 18:32 NIV

*If David had not suffered, would he have written the Psalms?*

*Lord, may the suffering that comes into my life be a beacon light to those who know me, those who stand behind the scenes and watch. To attempt to impress others with my talents and achievements is a futile, worthless undertaking. Those things vanish like the early morning fog. But to share with others my knowledge of God so they can relate and then stand tall and know that God is their strength—yes, Lord, I want to do what David did. And even as I say that, I know I'm opening the door for suffering. I'll make it, though. David and I relate there, too. I've learned that You are my strength.*

**The Lord is my strength and my shield; my heart trusts in Him, and I am helped.**

PSALM **28:7**

# 43

## *From Fear to Trust*

We first noticed her in the backyard under the hedge—scared to death. She was actually trembling. How or why she had been mistreated was a mystery, but she was really skittish. She was also really hungry and lonesome, so she compromised. She stifled her fear just enough to let us *see* her, but she wouldn't let us touch her. And whenever we saw her—pathetic, frightened little creature—we fed her. She won the first round.

Her red hair was matted and dirty, but she looked pretty well-fed. (We didn't know until later that this well-fed look was due to her being "great with child"!) Our boys were patient. They didn't rush the relationship. They would just talk to her gently and give her tidbits. They called her "Friend." Eventually—after she'd decided that we were safe—she wound up sleeping on the back doorstep. She was literally covered with ticks and fleas, so we coaxed her into the car and took her for the full treatment at the vet. We won the second round.

Friend was the first longhaired dachshund I had ever seen, and her trip to the beauty shop was nothing short of miraculous. It opened our back screen door for her and made her world much wider and more comfortable, for she was soon sleeping on the kitchen floor. And so began our days with sweet little Friend.

She had her puppies, the first that our family had ever produced, and so we all acted pretty much like new fathers—hovering and talking and watching and wishing this uncomfortable, painful event would hurry up and be over. She had them in the middle of the night without our help. She won that round, too.

What a devoted little mother she was! Her every thought centered around those five demanding pups.

I remember the day I decided *I* should take over some of the mothering duties for Friend. It was dark and chilly in the garage, so I took the pasteboard-box bassinet with all the babies in it and set it out on the driveway in the sunshine. "Don't worry, Friend. This sunshine will be good for your babies. I'll help you watch over them."

Wade and I watched—got tired of watching—and disappeared back into the house from Friend's view. When we went out later, one of the puppies was gone! I panicked. *Oh, what have I done? I've always heard that male dogs will kill puppies. But I didn't hear anything. He was so little! How could he have climbed out of the box? What am I going to do?*

As always, my first response to the panic was to call Bill. "Have you prayed about it?" he asked. Well, that didn't exactly seem like the most *practical* step to take at the time, but Wade and I got down on our knees in the middle of the kitchen floor and prayed about Friend's problem.

Friend's problem? *I* was her problem. Her children, in her opinion, did *not* need sunshine and fresh air, and as Wade and I stepped out the backdoor we saw the "culprit" who was kidnapping the puppies. Friend had Chubby in her mouth, carrying him to the shadows and safety under the house. There were two others already there in the chilly darkness. Wade had to crawl under and retrieve them, and I carefully put them back in the garage. Friend won that round hands down.

The time came when the puppies didn't need a mother—they needed someone to romp and play with. So we had a "crazy puppy giveaway" up on the campus, and all of her little ones found homes where they would be loved and well cared for. Friend could finally relax and sleep on the kitchen floor.

She didn't live with us very long. She didn't live very long. And it was an unhappy Gillham brood that reminisced that first night without Friend. . . .

"Do you remember how scared she was when she first came?"

"Remember how the ticks started falling off? They were crawling around on the back doorstep."

"Well, we didn't have her very long, but she was sure a sweet little dog, wasn't she?"

"Boy, I miss her."

Friend, in her quiet, gentle way won our love. But then we won her love too. We took care of her and stroked her and talked to her and let her sleep in the kitchen. . . .

*There are a lot of us like Friend—scared of You, Lord. We're all covered with unpleasant things and wonder if You will have anything to do with us. Some of us have glaring problems. But You don't run us off. You care for us, and sometimes You have to coax us to do things that You know will be best for us.*

*The wonder of it all is that You love us from the very beginning—when we're hiding in the darkness out under the hedge—and You don't stop loving us when we get close enough for You to see everything that's wrong with us. Why do we insist on limiting Your love to only beautiful people? You don't even look at the outside. You see the potential—what a trip to Your "beauty shop" will do for us.*

*Thank You, Lord, that You saw the potential in me. I certainly wasn't very lovely, but You accepted me and patiently cared for me.*

*And I finally understood that You were safe.*

# 44

## *Sometimes I Wonder*

*When I awake in heaven, I will be fully satisfied, for I will see You face-to-face.*

PSALM **17:15** TLB

Seeing You "face-to-face."

I will, no doubt, be beside myself. My heart will be racing and I'll be nervous and awfully excited—"all a-flutter."

I've read books about the early pioneer days and how ordering a bride by mail was a common practice. I can imagine how "all a-flutter" a woman would be as she was on the last leg of her journey, riding the stage into the town where her new husband would step up and claim her as his bride. Oh, they would have been corresponding and would know a lot about each other, but seeing him face-to-face would be nothing short of emotional basket-weaving—in and out and up and down and around and over the top and through the bottom and in and out. . . .

*Lord, I don't want You to misunderstand me. I'm anticipating that time when I'll see You face-to-face, and*

*I know within my heart that it will be more wonderful than I can possibly imagine.*

*But sometimes I wonder. . . .*

*You are so precious to me today. The way we walk and talk together. And I don't have to share You with anyone else. You are constantly with me—as close as my every breath. When I can't go to sleep, I talk to You. You're there. When I'm all alone and singing love songs to You, You're listening. (You are so polite.) You've kept every tear I cried in a bottle. These things bring me so close to You.*

*Will our relationship be as sweet in Heaven?*

I won't need You then as I need You now.

I won't rush to You for comfort and
   understanding.

I won't need to talk to You about my problems.

There'll be huge crowds vying for Your
   attention . . . and You know how I am about
   crowds—I just won't go rather than get in a
   shoving match with a bunch of people.

Will You still hold my hand?

Can I still snuggle down in Your lap when
   things go wrong? (But things won't be
   "going wrong" in Heaven, so I won't need
   to sit on Your lap, will I?)

I like to close my eyes and climb the mountain with You when You isolate Yourself for prayer. And we won't be doing that anymore.

I like the story about your walking with the men on the road to Emmaus—just strolling and talking.

*Well, those are my thoughts; and as You can see, there's a lot of insecurity there for me, Lord. You're my best Friend. You are my Confidant, my Protector, my Knight in shining armor. You know, I've got a good thing going here, and I don't want to lose it.*

*Maybe I should look at this dilemma and answer myself the way I used to answer the boys when they would ask, with teary eyes, if our latest beloved dog that had come to an untimely end would be in Heaven.*

*I'd say, "You are going to be so happy in Heaven—and if having Esther (or Dutch, or Grundoon, or Gretchen, or Zeke, or Zoro) with you will make you happier, then God will see to it that you have Esther."*

*I guess what I had better do is make the most of the time I have with You now, believing that I'll have everything I need to be "so happy" when I finally see You face-to-face.*

# 45

## The True Battle

How I pray that these thoughts will be a source of strength *to* you, *for* you, and *through* you (and all of those are different). Ponder them carefully, prayerfully. Listen, the Lord is talking to you. . . .

*Do you see that the Life in you that the enemy longs to crush is the same as it was when I threw him from Heaven? His battle is against Me—you are the battleground.*

*I am conforming your soul into the likeness of Christ. Because Satan, as the Deceiver, knows what that will mean for him, he uses all of his resources against that goal of Mine. He attacks through whatever circumstance he can to defeat My plan and so keep you from setting your mind on My provision for the battle. His goal is to keep you from becoming conformed to the image of My Son and to keep you from walking by faith.*

*You are no threat to Satan as you accept his lies and temptations, but as you come closer and closer to the image he battles more intensely. His goal is and always has been to crush Jesus Christ. That is why I provided a way for you to die and be "born again," thus creating your New Life in Christ Jesus. He is the One who will do battle. But you must let Him and trust Him.*

*Dear One, you are My creation. I dwell within you. You must begin to realize:* The battle is Mine, not yours! *I have delivered you.*

*Your salvation is in Christ Jesus . . .*

*His Life in you is your victory . . .*

*His strength is what will win the battle that rages against your mind as the enemy seeks to destroy—longs to destroy—the temple of God . . . YOU!*

# 46

## Set Free by God's Truth

*How could I have been so stupid?*
*Why, oh why did I do that?*
*What a loser I am!*
*When am I going to learn?*
*How long is God going to put up with me?*
*I'm still stumbling around and causing all sorts*
    *of problems.*
*Time and time again I fail.*
*I'm sick of myself and the things that I do.*
*I just want to give up!*
*I'll never change.*
*I'm just kidding myself to think that I could*
    *ever . . .*

Stop! Where are all of those destructive thoughts coming from? Who's talking to me? Something's going on here that doesn't ring true. Sure. I was wrong. I failed and I confess that readily. But this is carrying things too far.

\* \* \*

*Do not rejoice over me, O my enemy.
Though I fall I will rise [again]; Though I
dwell in darkness, the Lord is a light for
me.*

MICAH 7:8

Okay, I blew it! I was wrong!

But don't you try to convince me that God is through with me. He's not going to give up on Anabel. He's the One who saved me in the first place. Don't you suppose He knew what He was getting into with me? He knows everything about me—past, future, and present, and He still loves me—*unconditionally!*

And I am NOT a loser! I'm a new creation in Christ Jesus. I just haven't learned how to walk like who I really am yet. But I will. One of these days I'll be running instead of stumbling and falling—and I'll win! You'll see.

So you just go back to your lair and shut up, Satan! Even though I've fallen (and will undoubtedly fall again) you don't need to think I'm down to stay. Don't gloat over me, my enemy. It may look pretty bleak right now, but I'll make it . . . because of the Lord. He lives within me and He loves me and nothing I can do will ever damage that love. Furthermore, He has told me, "Anabel, you *will* stand. I Myself will cause you to stand" (from Romans 14:4).

✻ ✻ ✻

Sound theology is my only key to real hope.

Satan, the Deceiver, is a liar, and a very persuasive and convincing liar (John 8:44). How many times I have listened to his insidious accusations and allowed them to separate me from the One who loves me, who can help me. . . .

*Lord, I don't want anything to come between us. The knowledge of You and the awareness of Your presence is my most precious possession. How wise of the Evil One to try to drive a wedge that would separate me from You.*

*Truth is my most powerful weapon. You have said, "You shall know the truth, and the truth shall make you free. . . . If therefore the Son shall make you free, you shall be free indeed" (John 8:32, 36).*

I'm free to be lovely
to be hateful and ugly
I'm free to stand or to fall.

I'm free to be sinful
to be headstrong and willful
I'm free to not sin at all.

So who makes me free
who gives me strength
how do I accomplish this feat?

I give Christ my life
Regardless of cost
Then rest in His love—complete.

He takes me and loves me
molds me and shapes me
To His image—beauty divine.

And all that He did
And all that He promised
Through His life and His death becomes mine.

# 47

## Follow Me

**He said to him, "Follow Me!"**

JOHN 21:19

"Peter, the time is coming when you will grow old and someone will force you to go where you don't want to go. But don't concern yourself with this, Peter. You will glorify Me in your death.

"In the meantime, Follow Me."

"But Lord, what about John?"

"What difference should that make to you? He may be around longer than you are, maybe even until I come again. Peter, keep your focus on yourself. You follow Me" (John 21:18–22 my paraphrase).

Dear Peter. Isn't it so easy to relate to him? He didn't think about what to say before he said it. He just blurted it out—"What about John?"

*It's fairly plain to me, Lord, what You were trying to get across to him: The important thing is that I follow You. That I not look at others to see how You're leading them or using them. That I don't try to analyze how You're working in their lives or what their relationship with You might be like. Focus on myself . . . I am to follow You .*

That pretty well takes care of my todays and my tomorrows, doesn't it?

And when death comes? "This He said, signifying by what kind of death [Peter] would glorify God" (John 21:19). I don't know what kind of a death I'm going to die, but whatever comes, I'm to glorify Him in it and through it.

*You know, Lord, I doubt my ability to do either of those things: to follow You today, or to glorify You in my death when it comes sometime tomorrow.*

"I don't recall having told you that it was up to you, Anabel. Remember, you are under the New Covenant, and I have come to live within you for the express purpose of meeting life—and death—*for* you. I too would doubt your ability to do these things yourself, dear one. That's the very reason the covenant takes care of this. I do not doubt *My* ability, so why not let Me handle it all for you?

"Follow Me, Anabel."

# 48

## *Standing Strong in the Face of Death*

Consider these thoughts carefully.
Think slowly. Deliberately.

What one thing do we seem to *fear* more
than anything else?
DEATH

Would God desire to teach us *not* to fear death?
YES

How could He teach us—show us how to meet this
fearful event—most effectively?

(*Before you read my suggestions, think of your own
plan for taking the sting out of this most-feared
experience for His children.*)

By allowing some of His most choice servants—including
His Son—to *experience* death . . .
meeting it with peace
with gentleness
with dignity
with hope
with strength and
with victory.

And while we observe—watching them stand bravely—
our fear would begin to diminish
and would be replaced with peace
with gentleness
with dignity
with hope
with strength and
with victory.

So when that time comes *I too will stand*,
for He has said to me . . .

**And stand [you] will, for the Lord is able to make [you] stand.**

**ROMANS 14:4**

# 49

## *Evidence of God's Love*

My dear Lord,
You have proven Yourself
in my life in times past . . .
Your strength
Your provision
Your love.
I am unaware of any of these
facets in my being just now.
(Even Your love seems so . . .
questionable.)

I accept what I have learned
in times past,
not what I am experiencing
at this moment,
and I say
(with trembling heart, ravaged emotions,
and confused mind)
I trust Your wisdom,
Your planning,
Your strength,

*asking You only to manifest*
*Your love to me in*
*some way. . . .*

* * *

*I felt Your touch on my cheek as I walked . . .*
     *the breeze*
*I received Your beautiful love gifts . . .*
     *the tiny flower*
     *the new growth on the trees*
     *the sky*
     *the dove*
     *the many sounds of morning.*

*Thank You for showing Your love to me.*

# 50

## *A Stubborn Little Lamb*

*As for God, His way is blameless.*

**PSALM 18:30**

*For the Lord your God is a compassionate God.*

**DEUTERONOMY 4:31**

*Whom He foreknew, He also predestined to become conformed to the image of His Son.*

**ROMANS 8:29**

*I am confident of this very thing, that He who began a good work in you will perfect it.*

**PHILIPPIANS 1:6**

"C'mon, Buttons, you can do it! Jump! Hey, you're supposed to go *over* the poles—not try to knock them down with your head! Jump! Please jump!"

Sherrie watched as the lamb tried every way to get around or under the hurdle rather than to jump over it. He was dirty and completely exhausted, and she was dirty and completely exhausted.

It was only three months until the first competition, and this stubborn Buttons adamantly refused to do what she knew must be done in order to win. She picked him up and *put* him over the barricade. She guided him through her legs and arms, making a tunnel that would be his *only* way to go. No success. She was dealing with an obstinate, stupid, rebellious little sheep.

This wasn't the first time Sherrie had entered a lamb in the livestock show, but it *was* the first time she had experienced such difficulty in training an animal that was bent on bucking someone so much bigger and smarter than he was. And she wasn't doing anything that would hurt him . . . only what it would take to make him into a prizewinning sheep.

Sherrie had tried everything to get him to go through this simple routine that was needed to strengthen his hindquarters. It was an important point in the judging, so she was obviously going to have to take more drastic measures. She had put his food on the other side of the hurdle and the silly little lamb still balked. In fact, he nearly wore himself out trying to get *under* the hurdle.

What to do? "Well, I'll just put in more barriers to where he can't possibly get under the barricade or go around it. He will *have* to go over it! Why he's so determined to go against what I have planned for him, and where he got it into his little brain that I'm trying to hurt him or that I'm doing something that will ruin his life, is beyond me."

*All of us like sheep have gone astray,*
*Each of us has turned to his own way.*

ISAIAH **53:6**

*Hummm. I think I understand a little better now why we're sometimes compared to sheep in Your Word.*

*My head is throbbing from trying to knock my problems out of the way. I'm weary. Exhausted. Bewildered. And why am I so determined that what You allow to come into my life is meant to hurt me or to wreck my plans, when Your only purpose is to make me into a prizewinning sheep?*

*I'm sorry, Lord. Thank You for working so hard with me. And I'm very thankful to know that You aren't going to give up on me.*

*My sheep hear My voice, and I know them, and they follow Me.*

JOHN **10:27**

*Come to think of it, You're the only One who knows the date of the competition. Maybe You're working overtime on some of us?*

# 51

## *The Whole Weight of Your Anxieties*

You've probably completed this task, but just to seal it in your mind, would you do it again . . . my way?

**1 Peter 5:7**

*You can throw the whole weight of your anxieties upon Him, for you are His personal concern* (PHILLIPS).

*Casting all your anxiety upon Him, because He cares for you* (NASB).

*Let Him have all your worries and cares, for He is always thinking about you and watching everything that concerns you* (TLB).

THROW: to cause to fly through the air by releasing from the hand while the arm is in rapid motion.

CAST: to hurl with force.

LET: to allow; to permit; a command using an auxiliary verb: "Let him go."

\* \* \*

Do you have something you are anxious about? Something you're worried about?

Well, imagine yourself having wrapped up into a secure bundle that "something" that's worrying you. Go through every step: Find a box, get your wrapping paper, some twine, the scissors, and of course the Scotch tape. (Every time we were wrapping a package my sweet daddy used to say, "Anabel, what did we ever do without Scotch tape?") Of course, you'll have to reduce your problem in size, but that's all right. A marriage or a seventeen-year-old would be pretty hard to contain in a bundle!

Now it's all wrapped and tied. Pick a secluded meeting place—one of your choice. Go there mentally (or physically, preferably), carrying your package.

You will meet the Lord there. Don't worry about what He looks like. You'll recognize Him.

See? Over there. There He is. Go to meet Him. Now give the package to Him. No instructions are necessary. He already knows all about it.

Watch Him turn and walk away from you with the package under His arm. Are you going to run after Him and grab it back? Never! *It is His.* You just gave it to Him. Write down the exact time and the date when you *gave* Him "the whole weight of your anxieties."

You have just driven a "stake."

You have just put into your memory banks a time when you really gave Him your problem.

You have built a tiny altar where you and your God met and He lifted a burden from your shoulders. Don't forget it.

*I will meditate on Your precepts.*
*I will regard Your ways.*
*I will delight in Your statutes.*
*I will not forget Your words.*

PSALM 119:15,16 MY PARAPHRASE

# 52

## *Does It Really Work?*

This is a letter from someone who was hurting intensely—in a different way than you are hurting,
perhaps. These are the results as she carried through on
1 Peter 5:7. She read it. She believed it. She acted on it.

*Your note about tying up the package was just
great, Anabel. I thought of every concern and fear
about the disastrous situation I was in; what the
consequences might be, both positive and negative;
the kids, me, my husband; the years behind and the
tragic events of those years, the uncertainty of the
years ahead . . . so many dreams, so many hopes, so
many unknowns.*

*I boxed it all up (in my mind), put everything
in, wrapped it, and tied it securely. Then I actually
drove down to the beach. I met Jesus in a very secluded spot, gave it all to Him, and He walked off
with it.*

*I remind myself that He has it and I am not to
fret about it. When I do get uptight, I close my eyes
and I see again the picture of Jesus walking away*

*from me with that wrapped package under His arm. Relief springs up from within and I find myself rejoicing . . . way down deep.*

> *HE WILL BE AS REAL TO ME AS I ALLOW HIM TO BE.*

# 53

## My Anxiety, God's Consolation

**When my anxious thoughts multiply within me, Your consolations delight my soul.**

PSALM 94:19

*O Lord, the thoughts that plague me. Anxious thoughts about what's happening in my world and in the lives of the people who live in my world with me. And Lord, these anxious thoughts interfere with my relationship with You. Your sweetness. Your purity. Your compassion and kindness. Your faithfulness. Your power. Your peace. And this interference is what brings on my distress, my depression, my defeating thoughts.*

*In my Journal I have a section for prayer marked "Urgent." But every one of the things on that page I know unequivocally (leaving no doubt) I have entrusted into Your hands. Are they still urgent? Can't I trust You with those things? Am I still supposed to be anxious about them? I think it would probably be*

an affront to You if I kept putting them on your desk day after day with big red letters—URGENT!

And once I let those anxious thoughts into my mind, the travail of birth begins, because thoughts birth emotions. And the anxious thoughts multiply and the intensity of the birthing process increases . . . and so does the pain.

Please, Lord, give me the discernment to recognize the intent of these thoughts and the will and desire to refuse them entrance into my mind, where the dividing and multiplying tricks begin.

Your consolations—Your words of comfort, of strength, of purpose, of hope—yes, these will bring rest to my weary soul. They will bring peace and contentment, and I will delight in them. What I have to do is be sure I'm not putting the same file on Your desk that I plopped on there yesterday. Then I've got to believe that You're a very efficient Administrator and that You will not let things pile up that are important to the people under Your authority.

I see: Your consolations won't do me any good at all unless I think about them.

**I am convinced that He is able to guard what I have entrusted to Him.**

**2 TIMOTHY 1:12**

*Am I really?*

158

# 54

## *He Dwelt Among Us*

**Is not this the carpenter, the son of Mary?**
<br>**MARK 6:3**

- Jesus had a workshop. Do you suppose it was tidy?
- Did He find fulfillment in creating things with His hands? (How different from the worlds He created "in the beginning" . . . with just a word!)
- Did He have a carpenter's belt around His waist?
- Did He whistle while He worked . . . or hum?
- Did He ever smash His thumb? What did He do?
- Did Mary go out to the shop and brag on His work, or just sit and talk to Him? Take Him a glass of water when it was unbearably warm outside?
- Was He proud to be a carpenter?
- Were there blemishes at times that He had to smooth out?
- Did He make mistakes? Was every finished product perfect?
- Were His hands callous from holding His tools?
- Did He consider "making this stuff" a waste of time?

- Did He train His younger brothers? Was He a patient teacher?
- Did He give the money He made to Mary to help with household expenses?
- How long was Joseph with Him?
- Father and Son working together ... did they laugh? Did they have a good time? Did they embrace when they were happy?
- Did Mary kiss her Son, Jesus, goodnight?

This is the One who spoke the universe into existence! What must have gone through His mind, moment by moment, as He worked, the sweat running down His face? Isn't that amazing? To choose to limit Himself to living in the confines of an earthsuit. . . .

What a God! What a wonderful, magnificent God!

# 55

## *An Eagle's Flight*

*Do you not know? Have you not heard?*
*The Everlasting God, the Lord,*
*The Creator of the ends of the earth*
*Does not become weary or tired.*
*His understanding is inscrutable.*
*He gives strength to the weary,*
*And to him who lacks might He increases power.*
*Though youths grow weary and tired,*
*And vigorous young men stumble badly,*
*Yet those who wait for the Lord*
*Will gain new strength;*
*They will mount up with wings like eagles,*
*They will run and not get tired,*
*They will walk and not become weary.*

ISAIAH 40:28–31

*Do you not know?*

Haven't you learned this yet? I have tried so
many ways to teach you the simple truth of
resting in *My* strength. You are too strong to
need Me. As long as *your* strength endures,

you will clutch it to your breast. No. You do not *know* yet.

*Have you not heard?*
It cannot be that you have never heard this. Perhaps you've never been ready to receive it, but surely you have heard?

*The Everlasting God, The Lord,*
*The Creator of the ends of the earth,*
*Does not become weary or tired.*
The Lord, our Lord Jesus Christ, the One who created everything in the heavens and the earth, isn't like you or me. He doesn't get tired. He doesn't know what it is to be weary! Too often we make God out to be like us. Temperamental. Impatient. Difficult. Pressured.

No. We mustn't make God like us. We are like God—and are becoming more and more like Him as He works within us.

*His understanding is inscrutable.*
We can't begin to comprehend—even slightly— how deep His understanding is of each of us and everything that concerns us. I need that: understanding. Understanding that doesn't scold or condemn. Understanding that doesn't preach to me. Understanding that listens and tries to see things from my point of view. Understanding that speaks softly.

*He gives strength to the weary,*

> He watches carefully, and when He sees us getting weary, He supplies more strength. It's kind of like watering your plants. You watch them carefully, and at the slightest droop you give them a drink. He sees our slightest droop.

*And to him who lacks might He increases power.*

> He is always ready to empower us. He waits to be asked, but His power is always available to us.

*Though youths grow weary and tired,*

> You know how kids seem to have an unlimited source of energy? Well, even if one of them should falter, He is there with His boundless, infinite power.

*And vigorous young men stumble badly,*

> Even if a trained athlete or a very strong young man should stumble or trip badly, He's right there, ready to lift him up and infuse new energy into him. I'm not young and I'm not an athlete, but there's a wide variety of folks in between those two . . . where I fit.

*Yet . . .*

> I love God's conjunctions. He always gives us a way out or some unexpected hope.

*Those who wait for the Lord*
There's the word: *wait.* How hard that is to do! We know deep within that He will sustain us. We know that His wisdom is far beyond ours. We know that His love for us is the motivator and the restrainer in our lives. But even knowing all of that, "waiting" for Him is something that most of us can't—or refuse to—actually do.

*Will gain new strength,*
*Will mount up with wings like eagles,*
*Will run and not get tired,*
*Will walk and not get weary.*

* * *

*Lord,*
*Not only do I want all of these things, I need all of these things. An endless supply of strength, and not just shoring up the old strength that wears thin. New strength! And like an eagle. . . .*

Did you know that eagles don't fly in flocks, like other birds do? They fly alone. And they can fly 6000 feet above the surface of the earth. Imagine! An eagle soaring in the upper air doesn't have to worry about tunneling through mountains, or fording swollen rivers, or losing his sense of direction and getting lost in the dense forests.

Me? Like an eagle? How wonderful! Soaring in the upper air all by myself, looking down on the scary things but not fretting about them. That could be me. . . . *And Lord, to keep on—day after day after day—and not give out, whether it's a hectic "running" day or a "walking" busy day. You sustain me.*

*As usual, Lord, I realize that the choice is mine.*
*Would You teach me, please?*
*Teach me to wait?*

# 56

## *New—and Confident—in Christ*

*Just as you trusted Christ to save you, trust Him, too, for each day's problems; live in vital union with Him. Let your roots grow down into him and draw up nourishment from him. See that you go on growing in the Lord, and become strong and vigorous in the truth.*

COLOSSIANS 2:6,7 TLB

Bill had already gone down to the meeting. He was so pleased (and more than a trifle proud) of his newly elected position on the Oklahoma Education Association staff—Vice President! He had given me a "goodbye peck," opened the door to our room, and walked out without a moment's hesitation. He was on his way, with great anticipation, to meet his new employees, amuse them with his "funnies," and let them benefit from the words of wisdom that casually escaped from his lips. In other words, Bill was swimming in his element!

What he didn't know at the time was that his poor wife, Anabel, was finding it very difficult to open the door and head down the stairs for everyone to see—*that's Bill's wife*—or to interact with—*quiet little thing, isn't she?*

I took one, long, last look in the mirror, making sure everything was in place. I viewed my new, beige, polka-dot, "homemade" dress from all angles with a full-length image. Then I started for the door. With hand on knob I said to myself, "I am a pretty woman. I am not a dummy. These people are not going to be scrutinizing my every move, my every word, how I look, or my verbal skills." And with that brief lecture I opened the door and stepped out into the world. . . .

\* \* \*

That's a pretty scary way to leave the safety of the hotel room, isn't it? But that was the best I could do. That comprised my fragile "body of truth."

Body of truth? Those things I believed at that point in time would equip me for facing the "Mondays" of my life. I had tried a lot of things. Discarded a lot of things. Settled on a few. And those few kept me going.

How different it is today. Oh, I still have my body of truth, but it isn't fragile, it isn't bent all out of shape when things don't go right. It doesn't depend on whether I'm a "pretty woman" or if I can hold my own conversationally in *any* group. No. It depends on one—and only one—performance act on my part: What I have done with Jesus Christ. The moment—the split second—that

I accept Him as my Life—*my* way of life—then He gives me an *unshakable body of truth.*

According to Him, that old, scared Anabel died in Christ (Galatians 2:20), and I was reborn "not of blood, nor of the will of the flesh, nor of the will of man, but of God" (John 1:13). I became *someone new* when I was born again (2 Corinthians 5:17), and the life of Christ became my life (Colossians 3:4). Furthermore, I was transferred out of the kingdom of darkness and into the kingdom of light (Ephesians 5:8; Colossians 1:13). I'm different! I'm new! And as this new creation in Christ, that old "body of truth" I walked in for years is *no longer me.*

*Try walking out of your hotel room now, Anabel!*

It works every time! I'm rather amazed at myself and how well "I" handle the pressures today that used to be much like walking up the stairs to the hangman's noose! Now I wish I could say that my emotional condition has improved as markedly as my belief system. Not so. But my emotions have difficulty "thinking"—remember?

One of these days, maybe they'll catch up.

# 57

## *Who Is Your Strength?*

**They will be held guilty, they whose strength is their god.**

HABAKKUK 1:11

God's characteristics—His immutability, His omnipotence, His omnipresence, His omniscience—were, of course, available for me and to me, but I was holding up pretty well with my own immutability, omnipotence, omnipresence, and omniscience.

You see, I had performed all my life to gain acceptance from others, and I had really been quite successful. I always looked to Anabel as the "author and finisher" of my strength.

### Omnipotent

I was powerful. I could do it! In fact, I used to say that by the time I was 22 years old I had learned two things very well: 1) I can learn; and 2) once I know how, I can do it. Nothing was too difficult for me to undertake. Oh, I might *hesitate* to accept the task of washing windows on the Empire State Building, but then out of my

*169*

mouth would come the all-too-familiar words: "Of course, I'll do it."

### Omniscient

I was wise. On the Dean's honor roll. Who's Who. I knew what I needed, what I wanted—and I had the tenacity to keep performing until I got it. That didn't wane as I became a part of the "real" world, either. I left college with my tennis racquet under my arm and a tank filled with self-sufficiency. I moved away from the protection of my loving parents, the familiar streets of dear old Poteau, and the comfortable life of home. I didn't have a placard around my neck, but it was emblazoned in my thought-life: *I can do it!*

### Omnipresent

I was on the scene—God wasn't. His omnipresence didn't impress me all that much. I needed physical proof of His presence, and I didn't have it. So I depended on the strongest person I knew . . . Anabel.

### Immutable

As far as being immutable—unchangeable—I was able to meet life, to roll with the punches and change if it was needed. I was in control. Why should that change? I was certainly not going to *stop* performing.

God's constant presence?

God's wisdom?

God's power?

Those attributes weren't doing me one whit of good, and since my own strength was what I depended on, by definition *my* strength was my god.

Let's just say that my attitude was, "I'll call You if I need You, God." And I never really thought through that mindset. You see, what I was saying (ignorantly . . . thankfully) was this: "God, I have learned to do this, this, and this quite well. I'm still working on this one, but You're helping me and pretty soon I'll get the hang of it. Now this one is still real hard, but if You'll just keep working with me I'll eventually conquer it, too; and then guess what, God? I won't need You at all!" (How presumptuous of me!)

After years in an unhappy marriage, after having a profoundly retarded son, after financial frugality that seemed to take the joy out of life, after dealing with the unpleasant people that I couldn't control or make go away . . . *I began to need Him.* I began to realize, for the first time in my life, that my strength was not working. My life was changing me from "the leading female role" to an introverted behind-the-scenes stagehand. In fact, I pretty much lost all interest in going to the plays. The performer was about at the end of her ability to perform!

Then I came across Habakkuk 1:11, and it was as real to me as Saul's encounter with Jesus on the road to

Damascus. That came, of course, after years of performing and after more pathetic years of failing. But even then there was still enough life in this strong woman to "kick at the goads!" I couldn't kick much longer, though. I was just too tired of trying.

Well, *today* I have a new verse, a new theme song: *The woman who has come to know that You are her strength is a woman who is blessed* (Psalm 84:5–7).

I've come to *know* this, but it was a very difficult lesson for me to learn. I had played "god" for a long time and was loathe to give up control. I was so sure of my ability. But God, through His patience and wonderful guiding hand in my life, brought me to the point where I can say very comfortably with Paul, "Not that we are adequate in ourselves to consider anything as coming from ourselves, but our adequacy is from God" (2 Corinthians 3:5).

Who is your strength?

# 58

## Daisies Don't Lie

*I was depressed—dejected—disillusioned. I had just found out that John Riley didn't love me. How? Oh, the very best way—pulling petals off a daisy. Daisies don't lie. It was obvious that he preferred Mary Jo to me. I had known it all along. But this was the coup de grace!*

Remember doing silly little things like that? A rose or a carnation wouldn't do. A chrysanthemum would be all right. But the very best was the daisy. Best for pulling the petals off one by one and settling the issue of whether he loves me or he doesn't love me.

> He loves me
> > He loves me not
> He loves me
> > He loves me not . . .
> and with each petal that flutters down
> we go from floating on fluffy "cloud nine"
> to being lower than the proverbial "snake's belly."

Do you remember? And every so often we would cheat to make sure that the test ended like we wanted it to end. We'd pull two petals off at one time, or forget (conveniently) where we were and pick up again on the positive instead of the negative. Child's play.

* * *

But I wonder: Did you ever use a daisy to decide whether God loved you or not? It's easy. It's true. It's wonderful. And I highly recommend it! There's one major difference, though: *The issue has been settled.* Go ahead, pull the petals . . .

> He loves me . . . (whisper)
> He loves me . . . (close your eyes and say it)
> He loves me . . . (can you comprehend that?)
> He loves me . . . (more than you could imagine)
> He loves me . . . *me!* (amazing)
> He loves me.
> *He loves me* . . . (He *really* does).

By the time you have a naked stem in your hand, the tears will be rolling down your cheeks and you'll be declaring to the whole world . . .

> *He loves me!*
> *He loves me!*
> *He loves me!*

# 59

## *An Instrument of God's Peace*

*Lord,*
*Make me an instrument of Your peace.*
*Where there is hatred, let me sow love,*
*Where there is injury, pardon,*
*Where there is doubt, faith,*
*Where there is despair, hope,*
*Where there is darkness, light,*
*Where there is sadness, joy.*

*Grant that I may not so much seek*
*to be consoled as to console,*
*to be understood as to understand,*
*to be loved as to love.*
*For it is in giving that we receive,*
*It is pardoning that we are pardoned,*
*And it is in dying that we are born to eternal life.*

How many times I've read or quoted or prayed the prayer of St. Francis of Assisi . . .

*Lord, make me an instrument of Your peace.*

That's the first line, but then he goes on with how he desires to be used as an "instrument." I began thinking about what I was reading, and quoting, and praying. An instrument—let's say a musical instrument. What's unique about it?

Well,

> it can be picked up or put down
> it can bring forth beauty and loveliness or it can
> bring forth harshness, discord, and dissonance
> if it's well made, it makes a prettier sound
> it's useless without someone to play it
> the more talented or gifted the person is who
> plays it, the lovelier the sound and the more
> successful the performance

*You, Lord, You must make me an instrument of Your peace—that's beyond my capability. Oh, I can try, but You know very well that it will be a hit-or-miss proposition. I'll say something hateful and hurt someone or get hurt, or tired, or frustrated, and there will go all my "music." But how wonderful it is to be fashioned and used by You to bring beauty and love and harmony into my world. I want to be Your instrument.*

And why "peace"? Why did St. Francis believe it was so important? Is it "relevant" in our world today?
Yes.

You see, as an instrument of His *peace,* instead of *react-ing* to hate, I *respond* with love. I have the wisdom and power to do that because of the *peace* that I experience as Christ lives in and through me.

Pardon produces *peace,* and not until I have pardoned will I have *peace.*

Faith nurtures *peace,* and only faith can plant the seed of *peace.*

Hope gives birth to *peace,* for as I set my mind on "hope," I will have *peace.*

Light reveals *peace,* for if you are filled with light within, with no dark corners, then the outside will be radiant too, as though a floodlight were beamed upon it (see Luke 11:36).

Joy releases *peace.* How often I have found that as I give voice to joy, then *peace* is released.

If I do not demand consolation, understanding, and love for myself, but seek to give these to others, *peace* will be the result. If I give, I will be at *peace.*

If I die, then the Lord can use me as an instrument of His *peace.*

*Lord, You tell me in Romans 6:13 that I choose either to present the members of my body to sin as instruments of unrighteousness, or to God as instruments of righteousness. To be picked up and used by sin or to be picked up and used by You . . . why, there's no*

*debate. There is nothing to discuss. I choose to pre-
sent myself to You.*

*So once again, I read or I quote or I pray . . .
Lord, make me an instrument of Your peace—please.*

# 60

## *The Walk of Faith*

This is just *driving the stake down deeper* . . .
and a deep foundation brings greater stability.

**My calmness must be in the knowledge of God's
presence . . . not in the manifestation of His power.**

*Covenant of Peace*

I *know* . . .
Christ is dwelling *in* me.
Christ is my very *life*.
*I have given* my burdens to the Lord.
This time on earth is a temporary experience—
a *learning experience*.
Christ, dwelling *in* me as my very *life*, can meet my
today as well as what lies behind and ahead of
me with victory, calmness, and wisdom.
My *only* hope of meeting each circumstance in my
life with stability and serenity and wisdom is
to allow *Him* to meet each circumstance
*through* me. This is a *faith* walk, and faith is
rooted in the mind, not in the emotions.

I am a new creation. I am loved and accepted. I am *in* Christ. Resting. Secure. Empowered.

I enter into this covenant agreement with the Lord on this date:_____

Signed: _____

*"The mountains may be removed and the hills may shake, but My lovingkindness will not be removed from you, and My covenant of peace will not be shaken," says the Lord who has compassion on you.*

**ISAIAH 54:10**

# 61

## Guard and Fight

*He was a murderer from the beginning, and does not stand in the truth, because there is no truth in him. Whenever he speaks a lie, he speaks from his own nature, for he is a liar and the father of lies.*

**JOHN 8:44**

Do you realize that Satan, the Deceiver, is completely unethical, totally evil, incapable of telling the truth, and unbelievably cruel—and that he will hit you the hardest when you are down?

Do you realize that when you are under stress, when you are not at your best emotionally or physically—you're tired and don't feel well—this is when he will initiate his most diabolical schemes in your life?

Are you just a tad apprehensive about this?
Well, what do you do?

Most importantly, you don't listen to the lies he whispers to you, the thoughts of failure, bitterness, rejection, hurt—whatever they might be. Remember, he gives you those thoughts with first-person, singular pronouns—you will think they are *your very own thoughts!* No, they aren't.

You must be alert to Satan's devious methods.

Guard the entrance to your mind.

Carefully examine every thought that comes.

Control your thought-life.

Exert force.

Say "NO! I refuse that thought."

> *Fix your thoughts on what is good and true and right. Think about things that are pure and lovely, and dwell on the fine, good things in others. Think about all you can praise God for and be glad about.*
>
> PHILIPPIANS 4:8 TLB

You don't think you can do that?

You are *so* right.

Neither can I.

*We* can't. *You* can't.

But *you can* (even though your system may be all messed up) when you remember where your strength comes from, because *His* victory is *your* victory.

Difficult? Very.
Your choice? Yes.
Results? Victory or defeat—depending on your
  choice.

*Fight, dear one, fight.*

# 62

## The Other Side of the Fence

Shotzie stood on the top step and surveyed his world proudly, but cautiously. He didn't see anything out of the ordinary, so he leisurely descended the six steps and began exploring his territory. Everything was going just fine until he stepped into the cul-de-sac. Then he heard her coming, but by then it was too late. He knew he couldn't attempt a fast getaway on his short legs, so he braced himself as best he could for the broadside blow he knew was coming. He had suffered through it before, to his deep humiliation.

How did he miss her? Where had she been hiding? Why did she insist on picking on him? He had never done anything to her. Well, tomorrow he'd just have to be more careful, or maybe stay in the house all day.

Shotzie was a dachshund. His enemy? An eighteen-pound terrier. My sweet little Esther Lou. Why she took this instant dislike to her little German neighbor was beyond me. She had no enemies. She was a lover. A lover to everyone, that is, except poor little Shotzie.

I remember one day vividly. I was in the backyard with Esther. She was lounging in the sun while I repotted some plants. Suddenly she was a barking ball of black fury heading for the fence. Shotzie was on her turf!

The dachshund was terrified! He froze. Then he realized that Esther was behind the fence, and how he did strut. He actually had the nerve to hoist his short little leg and mark *her* territory! He came right up to the fence and she couldn't do a thing about it. She kept trying to intimidate him with growls and snarls and all sorts of war maneuvers. Nothing worked. Shotzie's nemesis was powerless. I can well imagine that his heart was beating furiously, that his minature legs were pretty wobbly, and that he was fighting a panic attack that was violently urging him to retreat. NOW! But no. Shotzie wasn't about to retreat. You see, he *knew* something about his enemy. *Esther was powerless.* Shotzie was merely taking advantage of the fence.

\* \* \*

*Lord, how I need to learn from Shotzie, to scrutinize my enemy and to gather information about his position—to see him as he is: powerless to harm. Sure, he makes an awful lot of noise, dashing up and back and up and back, snarling and showing his teeth. And my legs may be wobbly and my heart beating like crazy. But I've got to keep my perspective.*

*He's on the other side of the fence.*

# 63

## When God Says No

*In the days of His flesh He offered up both
prayers and supplications with loud crying and tears to the One able to save Him
from death, and He was heard because of
His piety.*

**HEBREWS 5:7**

I've seen pictures and drawn the scene in my own
mind of Jesus offering up those prayers (Matthew
26:38–44)—intense, fervent, emotional, desperate, tear-
ful prayers. And we've just read that He was heard. But,
even though His prayers were heard, apparently they
*were not answered as He had petitioned*.

That seems incredible to me. If anyone should have
His prayers answered immediately and to the most
minute detail, it would be Jesus, the Christ, the Son of
God.

You know, that happens to me too. A crisis comes.
Difficult circumstances. I pray, and when the answer
doesn't come as I expected, all sorts of thoughts invade
my mind. *What do I do? Have I done something wrong?*

*Is my prayer not right?* The difficult circumstances that Jesus was facing were not changed despite His prayers. What did *He* do? What did *He* have to stand on?

• Well, He must have known that He was in God's plan. How can I say that? Because the plans were not altered, even though His prayers were heard when He suggested Plan B. Have you ever suggested to God that there might be a better plan, only to have Him apparently reject your suggestion? Have I? Yes, many times. Doesn't that mean that He has said, "No; My plan is better; we'll go with Mine"? Jesus stood on that, and so can we.

• He was assured of His ability to meet the circumstances because the circumstances were not changed. God is faithful. He will not give you more than you can endure (see 1 Corinthians 10:13). If He were not totally confident in my ability to endure, He would remove the circumstance. I can believe that and walk in it, and so can you.

• And how about this: He was *not* comforted by the knowledge of God's presence with Him. In fact He cried out, "Why are You not with Me? Why have You forsaken Me?" At the most crucial time—the most difficult time in His life—God left Him on His own. He abandoned Him. Have you ever cried out, "God, where are You when I need You so desperately?" Does He *ever* leave you or forsake you? No. We never have to experience what

Jesus did . . . because of what Jesus did! "Even when we are too weak to have any faith left, He remains faithful to us and will help us, for He cannot disown us who are a part of Himself, and He will always carry out His promises to us" (2 Timothy 2:13 TLB). That is ours! We can stand on that.

• He then proceeded on what He knew to be Truth and what He had come to know of God in days past, not on what He was experiencing at the moment. Isn't that walking by faith? "For we walk by faith [we regulate our lives and conduct ourselves by our conviction or belief respecting man's relationship to God and divine things, with trust and holy fervor; thus we walk], not by sight or appearance" (2 Corinthians 5:7 AMP). Oh, the circumstances may be intense and they may not change, but I know God. I've walked with Him through the years. So I will proceed in what I have come to believe.

That door of faith was open to Jesus, and it is open to us.

• His prayer was heard "because of His piety" (meaning godly reverence), not because of who He was, not because of His outstanding miracles, but because of His "godly reverence." Do you understand? This piety, this godly reverence that brought about answered prayer, can be ours just as it was His.

• This one act of sacrifice was the final proof of His worthiness. "It was after he had proved himself perfect in this experience that Jesus became the Giver of eternal salvation to all those who obey him" (Hebrews 5:9 TLB).

He had fulfilled the plan. From the very beginning He set His face like flint toward Calvary (Isaiah 50:7). He refused to be deterred.

"For who knows but that this is the very reason that you came to earth? For just such a time as this, for this very hour?" (Esther 4:14 my paraphrase). Like Queen Esther, like Jesus, maybe God's plan for *us* involves "such a time as this." Quite a high calling. Can I accept that high calling? Yes, I can, by His grace and strength. So can you. Like Jesus and so many saints over the centuries, we can stand on these truths . . .

- God's will—God's plan—is supreme. I will rest in God's will.
- God will not allow something to come into my life that I cannot bear.
- It may seem like He is far away, but He has promised that He will never leave me.
- I *know* the Lord. He loves me. I will walk by faith in that truth.
- He hears my prayers because of my love for Him.
- This may be the one experience in my life for which I was created. I certainly don't want to blow it!

*I watched You, Lord, when You were facing circumstances of a magnitude that I have not experienced. I listened to Your prayers. I walked by Your side. I learned. Thank You, dear Jesus, for showing me the way through this maze of hurt, confusion, and unrest.*

# 64

## The Perfect Peace of God

**I will give you perfect peace if you will stay your mind on Me.**

ISAIAH 26:3 MY PARAPHRASE

The door had just closed behind Wade . . . the last one to leave with his lunch sack under his arm. Bill was gone. Even Esther, our dog, was outside. And I was getting ready for another big round of depression. I had made it through breakfast and fixing lunches, but now that I was alone I was going under . . . *fast.*

I had been pacing the house and was walking down the hallway when, in utter frustration, I stopped, made a fist, and shook it in God's general direction. (I'm confident He was very impressed.)

*God! You have promised me peace, and I don't have it! I am an emotional basket case. My insides are churning. My hands are trembling. My thoughts are so confused that I don't know whether I'm coming or going. There's a lump in my throat that just stays there. I am hurting so badly, and I certainly* don't have any <u>semblance</u> of peace! My world is completely haywire! Why, Lord, why?

And it was almost like He whispered to me . . .

"Anabel, what are you setting your mind on? What are you thinking about?"

* * *

How many times have you accused Him of being the reason for your problem, for not coming through on His end of the bargain? No. You must understand that He never promised an unconditional peace. It comes with instructions: *I will give you peace if you will stay your mind on Me.*

*I guess I'm a slow learner, Lord. I still think of peace*
*as freedom from problems. No. That's not it, is it?*
*Peace is resting in You. Peace is knowing You can*
*face the day through me.*
*Regardless.*
*I remember, Lord, when I used to wake up and say,*
*"My God! Another day! How can I possibly get*
*through it?" It's different now.*
*Oh, I still wake up and call on You, but I say,*
*"My precious God. Thank You that You are*
*going to meet today for me."*
*That's peace. Perfect peace.*

**I pray that this thought will cause you to rest more completely in His arms today.**

# 65

## A Lot Like Peter

*And He began to teach them that the Son of Man must suffer many things and be rejected by the elders and the chief priests and the scribes, and be killed, and after three days rise again.*

**MARK 8:31**

**Peter:**

*What?*

*Rejected? You? Such foolishness! The people love you! When was it that you fed the four thousand—just three or four weeks ago? Surely You don't think they've forgotten that! And since when have you heard of multitudes of people following after someone as they do You? Why, You're their only hope! What You can do for them is limited only by Your own choice, and they know that. They're not about to reject You!*

*And suffering? You are God's Messiah. He wouldn't plan for <u>You</u> to suffer. Besides that, You can control such circumstances. There is no reason why*

You should suffer unjustly. I don't know why You're talking like this.

And as if that were not enough You talk about being killed! That is completely incomprehensible! God would not do that to us or to You—You who taught us the ways of God—You who have shown us God as we never knew Him—You who have brought hope to us. For You to be killed would ruin all of our plans! This would be absolutely disastrous to the cause—to all the work that we have done! This just cannot be true. That's all there is to it.


**Jesus:**

Peter, you're looking at this from the wrong perspective. You're looking at it from a human point of view instead of from God's point of view. I know—God's ways are unfathomable, and you can't understand His ways. I agree. And yes, I am their only hope. But "hope" for what, Peter? Hope to eat again and not be hungry? Hope to walk again and not be crippled? Hope for release from pain? Ah, Peter. I am so much more than that! Hope for "today"? There is forever, Peter.

You see, you failed to mention the last thing—after three days I will rise again. That, too, is beyond your comprehension, isn't it? But I know the plans. My Father and I made them together. It's all right, Peter. Don't discourage me, My friend. I am very confident that I am exactly where God wants Me to be at this point in time.

193

**Anabel:**

*I do that, don't I, Lord? I mean that I look at things from a human point of view, thinking that God surely hasn't thought this thing through, and if He were just as astute as I am, He would do it my way.*

*You knew what was going to happen—all of it—and You still said, "I am confident that I am exactly where God wants me to be at this point in time." I don't know what's ahead, but I want very much to say with you, "I am confident that I am exactly where God wants me to be at this point in time."*

*Be patient with me, Lord. I want to learn. And—I love you.*

# 66

## A Letter from One Who Loves You

There are so many worlds open to us when we're little. The "dog days" of August can send us to lush jungles, fighting mosquitoes and headhunters; the narrow confines of our postage-stamp backyard can engulf all of Alaska, and our self-image becomes whatever we want our self-image to become.

When do we lose our capacity to "play-like"? Why is it so difficult for us to close our eyes and "just imagine" once we become adults? Is the world of imagination marked "Children Only"?

Let's pretend together. *Let's play-like.* . . .

You are married—happily married (which may be difficult for some of you even to *imagine*). Our country becomes entangled in a full-scale war. You and your husband agree that he should enlist, and so he does. Basic training lasts several weeks, and then he returns home for a brief time before being sent into active duty. How precious those few days are . . . and then he's gone. You hear from him regularly for a while, but then the letters stop coming. One finally does come, but it's not from him. It's from the United States Government:

*We regret to inform you that your husband has been taken as a prisoner of war. . . .*

Your husband's captors are lenient in one way: They are going to allow him to communicate with you. Once. They will permit him to write a single letter, restricting the number of pages he can use. Now, do you suppose he would write that one letter out in a flurry of scribbles? I don't. I imagine him making notes, jotting down everything he wants to say to you, remembering how you had depended on him, how you had valued his opinions and advice. He makes certain, as best he can, to anticipate your questions and the unexpected pressures that will undoubtedly arise in his absence. Then he requests permission to write his letter.

Imagine receiving that envelope . . . his writing. He's talking to you. He's alive. He loves you. Oh, it hurts terribly because he isn't here, but at least you have his words, his encouragement, his loyalty, his love. What are you going to do with that letter? Put it in a safe-deposit box at the bank . . . after you've made ten copies of it, that is.

His one message begins with *I love you and I miss you.* Then he writes, *Now, about the children . . . this is how you should work with them, and here are some suggestions for discipline. . . . Be careful with your finances, and don't co-sign any notes. By the way, I love you. . . . In dealing with the mortgage people, there are certain things you should be aware of. . . . Check*

*through your important papers to evaluate our insur-*
*ance coverage. . . . And by the way, I love you. . . .*

You read those pages over and over and over again.
You know right where to find that advice about finances
or the children, and you read the end of the letter every
night before you go to sleep: *I'll be coming back one of*
*these days. Wait for me. Watch for me. Be faithful to me.*
*I love you so much.*

❋ ❋ ❋

God's Word, the Bible, is His one love letter—His
one message—to you. There are paragraphs where He
gives you His thoughts on discipline; He talks about financial matters; there are pages concerning interper-
sonal relationships; and He gives advice on how to meet
the myriad unexpected pressures that will undoubtedly
arise in His absence.

He's alive! He has written to you! He loves you! He
tells you He's coming back one of these days: "Watch for
Me. Wait for Me. Be faithful to Me." Can you *imagine*
that? Incredible!

Years ago I saw a movie with Jennifer Jones and
Joseph Cotton. I believe it was called *Love Letters*. The
plot of the story wasn't that unusual: A soldier came to
town and swept the heroine off her feet with tender
words, gifts of love, and rash promises . . . then he left.
She wrote to him, but he wasn't interested in writing to
her. It had been nothing more than a weekend fling for
him. So he asked his roommate, Joseph Cotton, if he

would take on her letters as a project and answer them for him. Joseph agreed. Well, Jennifer fell in love with Joseph, the man who wrote her the love letters. The theme song is still around:

Love letters straight from your heart
keep us so near while apart
I'm not alone in the night
when I can have all the love you write
I memorize every line
I kiss the name that you sign
And then darling I read again
right from the start
Love letters straight from your heart.*

As you've read God's "love letter" to you, there are probably certain paragraphs so special that you've underlined them, highlighted them, or put an asterisk beside them; they linger like an old song. John chapter 14 is hopelessly dotted with highlights and ink marks in my Bible: verses 1, 2, 6, 13, 21, 26, 27, 31 . . . among the others.

I wonder if you have highlighted or underlined John 14:20, perhaps my most cherished promise in this chapter: "In that day you shall know that I am in My Father, and you in Me, and I in you." The Living Bible translates the same verse this way: "When I come back to life

---

*"Love Letters." Copyright © 1945 by Famous Music Corporation. Copyright renewed 1972 by Famous Music Corporation.

again, you will know that I am in my Father, and you in me, and I in you."

*In that day...when I come back to life again....* That is after the fact, the fact of His resurrection. Our faith stands on that fact. Romans 10:9: "If you confess with your mouth Jesus as Lord, and believe in your heart that God raised Him from the dead, you shall be saved." First Corinthians 15:14: "If Christ has not been raised, then our preaching is vain, your faith also is vain...."

Jesus said, "You shall *know* that I am in my Father, and you in Me, and I in you." Webster gives this definition for *know: to recognize as valid or as a fact; to perceive with understanding and conviction.* To know means to be convinced, certain, without a doubt, to understand fully.

One of the primary ways we come to *know* something is through experience, and how well I remember this one vivid learning experience: I was probably ten or eleven years old at the time, and I was cleaning up the kitchen after breakfast. We had used the toaster, and I (probably because I didn't especially want to be cleaning up the kitchen) used a little too much "jerk" when I unplugged the toaster. One of the little gold prongs broke off in the outlet. I was in for trouble unless I could right the wrong before Mother returned to the scene of the crime. I didn't know what to do (much less what *not* to do), so I took a fork. . . . Need I say more? I *knew* something after that experience, and I decided then and there I would never stick a fork into an outlet again.

"When I come back to life again, you will *know*" something, Jesus said. All right, Lord, what do I know now that You have come back to life? "You will know that I am in the Father, that you are in Me, and that I am in you." Just words, unless you'll do something with Me, unless you'll *come to know* with Me.

Go get three envelopes of graduated sizes and a small slip of paper. On the largest of the envelopes print *GOD*. On the next size down print *JESUS*. On the smallest of the three print your name, and then on your slip of paper print *JESUS*. Take your large GOD envelope and place your JESUS envelope inside it. Take the envelope with your name on it and place it inside the JESUS envelope. Now take the slip of paper with JESUS printed on it and drop it into that envelope with your name on it. "When I come back to life again, you will know that I am in the Father, that you are in Me, and that I am in you." What an amazing concept of God and His relationship with us! *Look where you are!*

Secure. Safe. Sheltered. Hidden. Surrounded by love. Do you see that *anything that comes into your life must first come through God and through Jesus before it gets to you? And when it gets there, it finds you filled with Jesus . . . so what is there for you to fear?* I'm not talking about "*feeling* afraid." Your emotions may be sky-rocketing and you're one more "straw" away from becoming an emotional basket case. No. I'm talking about *knowing* something. I know I am secure. I know I have nothing to fear. You set your mind on this truth, and your emotions will *eventually* respond.

How great is your God? Is anything too difficult for Him? Can anything come into your life that He cannot handle? No. What about the performance of others and its impact on you? Can Jesus handle that? Of course. What about *your* performance? Can loneliness, unhappiness, or abuse destroy you? No. *Because you know where you are,* can you rest in His love, in His wisdom, in His strength? Yes. We are *in the world*, and He has forewarned us that we will have "tribulation and trials and distress and frustration" (John 16:33 AMP); but if you will only remember where you are, you will be *more than a conqueror:* "But in all these things we overwhelmingly conquer through Him who loved us" (Romans 8:37).

I have no idea where you are right now, but wherever that might be, do you realize that you aren't alone? Do you realize how much He loves you? That He's coming back for you? Close your eyes and pretend, play-like, imagine the reality. You are nestled inside pockets of love with Jesus indwelling you as your very life—He said so in His love letter to you.

*Such boundless wonders are not limited to six- and seven-year olds.*

# 67

## *Grace and Peace to You*

MY NEEDS:

There are two things I need in my life right now. Only two. With these two things I will get through these difficult circumstances with at least a measure of victory.

*Need #1*: The ability to meet this situation head-on with some wisdom, some strength, some composure. I feel so completely inadequate, so frustrated, so hemmed in on every side. I simply cannot do it!

*Need #2:* Some relief from the pressure that is being exerted against me as I struggle with this issue. I am almost a basket case. I react to every little irritation that comes my way. I just really don't know how much longer I can take this stress!

Just those two things, Lord, just those two.

MY ANSWER:

> **May you know more and more of grace and peace *as your knowledge of God and Jesus our Lord grows deeper.***
>
> **2 PETER 1:2 PHILLIPS**

GRACE: God's power freely given to me to meet my circumstances.
>               (Provision for Need #1)

PEACE: Resting in God's GRACE.
>               (Provision for Need #2)

*   *   *

*Oh, Lord, I see! They're mine for the taking! These two things that I'm begging for, which I need so desperately in my life, are available to me as I spend time with You, getting to know You more deeply and more intimately. You, my Lord, are my answer.*

*Now, I should have known that. . . .*

# 68

## God's Perfect Timing

*I don't understand, God. I have prayed and prayed, and nothing has changed. I believe my prayers are within the scope of Your will . . . I'm not asking for anything amiss. What's wrong, God?*

**These things I plan won't happen right away. Slowly, steadily, surely, the time approaches when the vision will be fulfilled. If it seems slow, do not despair, for these things will surely come to pass. Just be patient! They will not be overdue a single day!**

HABAKKUK 2:3 TLB

Do you remember Zacharias and Elizabeth, the father and mother of John the Baptist? They didn't have John until very late in life. In fact, they had reached the age at which having children was highly improbable, if not impossible: "I am an old man, and my wife is advanced in years" (Luke 1: 18). But one day, while Zacharias was ministering to the Lord in the Temple, the angel Gabriel came to him and said, "Zacharias, your prayer has been heard."

Do you suppose Zacharias had been praying recently for a child? Do you think he was still entreating the Lord for a son? Maybe just yesterday in his prayers he had said, "O, Lord! Elizabeth and I are so very lonely. How we yearn to have a child. Please, Lord, bless our union and send us a baby. . . ."

I don't think so. I really don't think he had prayed that way for a long, long time. He had given up all hope that he would ever hear the patter of little feet around the house, for he was an "old man" and his wife was "advanced in years."

"Uh . . . what prayer is it that you have reference to, Gabriel?"

"The one you prayed years ago, Zacharias. Remember? You asked God for a son. You see, the fullness of time has now come, and the Lord is going to give you the desire of your heart—a son, Zacharias, a son!"

\* \* \*

*In the fullness of time. When is that, Lord? I don't really have any way of knowing, do I? Zacharias and Elizabeth had some lonely years . . . until the fullness of time when everything was ready . . . and then You fulfilled their prayer.*

God has an "appointed time" when every minute detail will be finished for you and for me. When that times comes, the prayer will be answered.

It may not be tomorrow
and yet it may
It will happen on God's set day.
The burden will be lifted
The lost one will be won
The trial will be over
The long task will be done.
We cannot know the hour
but we will trust Him as we wait,
for He knows just what must come to pass
He will not be a moment late!
So praise Him in the trial
give thanks for the task
rejoice and be obedient
He knows what you have asked.
It may not be tomorrow
and yet it may
It will happen on God's set day.

# 69

## *Our Children, God's Children* *

Lord, I come to You today to renew our covenant with regard to my beloved sons. The sons You gave me for my earthly family, but who are Yours . . . eternally. Your sons. Your family.

I relinquished all rights to them . . . gave them to You (Scriptures 1, 2) and, because of Your Word (and You cannot lie—3), I believe that You took what I lifted up to You. I am confident (4,8) that they are now in Your keeping (9,10).

How frightening it would be to think that You could not protect them. How insecure I would be if I doubted Your integrity, Your ability, Your loving care. How fearful if I never knew when the Deceiver was going to lure them out of Your grasp (i.e., Your back was turned and You didn't see him sneaking up). I can't imagine Your saying to me, very apologetically, "I just couldn't handle it, Anabel. I am so sorry."

You know each of them much better than I know them. Your love for them is much greater than my

---

* The Scriptures referenced are printed on the following pages. They—and only they—will make this covenant a "rock" that you can stand upon.

love for them. To whom could I give them who would take better care of them? You are God, and all that "God" means (11).

Believing this with all of my heart (12), I therefore make this statement: Anything (13) that comes into the lives of Pres, Will, and Wade must first come through God and through Jesus to get to them (14). They may not allow Jesus in them to take care of the situation, but God knew (10) before the foundation of the earth how they were going to handle it, and He is prepared to deal with them (15).

Thank You. I love You.

### Scripture References for "A Covenant"

**1. Psalm 55:22**
*Cast your burden upon the Lord, and He will sustain you; He will never allow the righteous to be shaken.*

**2. 1 Peter 5:7**
*Casting all your anxiety on Him, because He cares for you.*

**3. Titus 1:2**
*Which God, who cannot lie. . . .*

**4. Romans 4:20,21**
*With respect to the promise of God, he did not waver in unbelief, but grew strong in faith, giving glory to God, and being fully assured that what He had promised He was able also to perform.*

**5. Romans 14:4**
*And stand he will, for the Lord is able to make him stand.*

**6. Philippians 1:6**
*I am confident of this very thing, that He who began a good work in you will perfect it until the day of Christ Jesus.*

**7. Philippians 2:13**
*It is God who is at work in you, both to will and to work for His good pleasure.*

**8. 2 Timothy 1:12**
*I know whom I have believed and I am convinced that He is able to guard what I have entrusted to Him until that day.*

**9. Job 14:5**
*Since his days are determined, the number of his months is with Thee, and his limits Thou hast set so that he cannot pass.*

**10. Psalm 139:16 TLB**
*You saw me before I was born and scheduled each day of my life before I began to breathe. Every day was recorded in Your book!*

**11. Isaiah 46:9,10**
*I am God, and there is no other; I am God, and there is no one like Me, declaring the end from the beginning and from Ancient times things which have not been done, saying, "My purpose will be established, and I will accomplish all My good pleasure."*

**12. Mark 9:24**

*Immediately the boy's father cried out and began saying, "I do believe; help my unbelief."*

**13. Romans 8:28,29**

*We know that God causes all things to work together for good to those who love God, to those who are called according to His purpose. For whom He foreknew He also predestined to become conformed to the image of His Son, that He might be the firstborn among many brethren.*

**14. John 14:20** TLB

*When I come back to life again, you will know that I am in my Father, and you in me, and I in you.*

**15. Job 42:2**

*I know that Thou canst do all things, and that no purpose of Thine can be thwarted.*

# 70

## *A God Who Hears*

*The Lord has heard the voice of my weeping. The Lord has heard my supplication, The Lord receives my prayer.*

PSALM 6:8,9

*Blessed be God, who has not turned away my prayer, Nor His lovingkindness from me.*

PSALM 66:20

❈ ❈ ❈

My faith in this love of God has
become so sure that I abide in it
without question.

When my prayer is not answered
in the way I expected it to be answered,
it's all right.
I know I have submitted to a will
greater than my own and infinitely
more capable of making such decisions.
He is perfecting my prayer.

❖ ❖ ❖

*Not only have I submitted my will to You, I have relinquished all rights to my loved ones. Your will is my will for them. Keep them within Your will.*

*And should they stray from Your will for them, act quickly, decisively! You have my permission (as if You needed it!) . . . no, You have my urgent plea to do whatever You deem necessary to draw them back into Your way for them.*

*And thank You for listening.*

# 71

## *When Anger Overwhelms*

G od knows that confrontations and unpleasant circumstances are going to be a regular part of our
lives. But, as any loving authority will do, He gives us fair
warning—and then, through the Psalmist, gives us instructions on how to handle emotional crises.

> *Tremble, and do not sin;*
> *meditate in your heart upon your bed,*
> *and be still. Offer the sacrifices of righteousness,*
> *and trust in the Lord.*
>
> **PSALM 4:4,5**

TREMBLE:

"Your emotions will really cause you problems, Anabel. You may be so distraught that you will actually be
shaking! This can't be helped at times because you just
can't control your emotions. Besides that, your Adver-
sary may keep hitting at you until you are emotionally
undone. I understand that."

*God gives us the freedom to tremble.*

AND DO NOT SIN:

If you're making a salad dressing and the recipe calls for *1 tsp of salt and 1 tbsp of vinegar*, you don't have an option. Use *1 tsp* of salt, but do what you want to do with the amount of vinegar? No. It's part of the recipe. If you want it to turn out right, you follow the instructions. And if you don't follow them, it's your fault that it failed.

"Anabel, it's *okay* to tremble, but your emotions are not to control you. Don't sin. Don't vent your anger or say things you will be sorry you've said later on. Don't lash out. Don't physically do harm to yourself or to the one who has been badgering you (maybe it's the poor little cat under the table). Don't scream. Don't stomp around the room. Don't pout. Don't throw some kind of a tantrum. *Don't sin*. That's not an acceptable part of the procedure. You'll fail. It won't work. *You'll ruin the recipe.*"

MEDITATE IN YOUR HEART UPON YOUR BED:

The first thing to do is to isolate yourself. Go to the bedroom or the bathroom or the garage, or get in the car and drive down to the corner grocery. Get *alone.* Sit down and be quiet.

This meditation cannot be limited to thinking about the problem. If you set your mind on your problem, reliving it word for word, scene by scene, your emotions will stay up, or go even higher.

He instructs us to "meditate in your heart." We are to dig down deeply and examine what has been said and what has been done, using the light of our "new" heart—the heart that wants to please Him. The heart that has the laws of God written on it. The heart that is totally devoted to Him.

"Meditate from this view, Anabel, instead of how wrong he was, how hard you've tried, how you have been hurt, how long this has been going on, what she said, what you could have said, or any of those things."

*And instead, Lord?*

OFFER THE SACRIFICES OF RIGHTEOUSNESS:

A sacrifice is hard to make. It wouldn't be called a "sacrifice" if it were easy. There's nothing easy about it. A sacrifice of righteousness means acting righteous, thinking righteous thoughts, even if you don't "feel" like doing it.

Philippians 4:8 is not an option. It is not contingent upon our feelings. It is a command: "Fix your thoughts on what is good and true and right. Think about things that are pure and lovely, and dwell on the fine, good things in others. Think about all you can praise God for and be glad about" (TLB).

*But Lord! I am so upset! How can I set my mind on those things? I'm beyond rational thinking!*

At this point of emotional upheaval—brought about by anger or disappointment or distress of any kind, where my way has been thwarted—to think about the things listed in Philippians 4:8 will be a sacrifice of righteousness. I'll have to force myself to think those kinds of thoughts.

AND TRUST IN THE LORD:

Allow Him to step in, as any gallant knight would do, and protect you, taking on the "dragon"—let Him slay the monster before your astounded eyes! *Trust Him*.

Now, when someone comes to your rescue, what do you do? You thank him profusely, you praise his manly deed, and you cling to his arm.

*"I have just rescued you, Anabel.*
*Will you do this for Me?"*

# 72

## *When the Storm Rages*

*"Let us go over to the other side of the lake." And they launched out.*

LUKE 8:22

They were doing exactly what Jesus told them to do; and yet, by following His instructions, they set sail into a night that would be filled with terror.

And where was He? He was with them, of course. And don't you think He knew what was to come? He also knew that they were well-trained, competent, hardy boatsmen.

Well, their "competency" got a trifle shaky, to say the least, as the winds got stronger, tossing them down into the valley of one wave and throwing them up to the peak of another. And they could have kept on trying, yelling to each other, "We can do it! Hang on! We'll make it! It's slacking!"

But they chose another tack. Someone groped his way to the back of the boat, shook Jesus, and said, "Master! Wake up! We've got a big problem here! We're swamping."

Jesus calmed the waves first. Then He calmed them.

I know it would have pleased the Lord for one of them to have said, "Hey, you guys! Jesus is with us. We've all seen Him perform these mighty miracles, and we've got to rest in His presence during this storm. I'm scared just like you are. Scared to death. But He can handle it! Do you hear me? He can handle it!"

Oh, yes. They were aware of Him and His power and His authority much more intensely after He came to their rescue. They were "fearful and amazed, saying, 'Who is this? Even the winds and water obey Him!' " (from Luke 8:25). It was still a good experience. They learned and God was glorified.

I wonder, though, what Jesus would have said if the story had ended differently—if they had behaved differently. He seemed discouraged when He asked them, "Where is your faith?" I wonder if any of them understood.

*Lord, I would like to be a source of encouragement to You. I get awfully scared when the winds start knocking me around and my world is almost swamped, but I should know by now that You can handle it. Next time, Lord, I'll remember that night so long ago, and I'll say, "Think, now. Jesus is with us. We don't need to be afraid."*

*That doesn't mean my knees won't be shaking, right, Lord?*

# 73

## The Father's Discipline

**All discipline for the moment seems not to be joyful, but sorrowful; yet to those who have been trained by it, afterwards it yields the peaceful fruit of righteousness.**

**HEBREWS 12:11**

ALL discipline [*discipline of every kind*]
for the MOMENT [*when it is happening*]
seems NOT to be joyful [*not a happy thing, to say the least*]
but SORROWFUL [*difficult to handle or understand; depressing and wearisome*] yet to those who have been
TRAINED by it [*guided growth toward habitual behavior*]
AFTERWARDS [*think about that word*]
it yields the peaceful fruit of righteousness.

If a child accepts disciplinary action as
    necessary for maturing, for positive growth, and
    as coming from a base of love,
then *AFTERWARDS* the discipline will have been
profitable. She will have learned (been trained by it), and

positive growth will be the result. Don't we long for our children to understand this, to believe us, to know that our discipline comes from a base of love?

I'm just as sure that God longs for us to *understand* and believe that His discipline comes from an unfathomable reservoir of love for us. And if we respond accordingly, we will learn! We'll grow! We'll see the positive results of that discipline in our lives.

But, you know, there are alternatives to responding positively to His discipline:

## I CAN REBEL

"I was *not* wrong! You have no right to treat me this way. I resent Your interference and Your instruction, and I have no intention of going along with Your program. I'll do it *my* way, thank you."

## I CAN REFUSE

"So maybe I *was* wrong. But I refuse to change or say I'm sorry. I'm not that difficult to get along with—I think maybe You're disciplining the wrong person. What about him? What about her?"

## I CAN SIMPLY ENDURE

"Hey, I'll make it. I can handle this. You can't get a good man down and keep him there. I'll come back stronger and better! You keep it up, I'll keep it up. . . ."

*I CAN PASSIVELY ACQUIESCE*

"Oh well, you win a few, you lose a few. Into each life some rain must fall. Whatever will be, will be. . . ."

*I CAN RETALIATE*

"I'm not going to be a doormat for anyone. I have *my* rights. I'm a fighter! The name of the game is *survival,* and I intend to survive!"

Then there is, of course, the *POSITIVE* response:

"I'm sorry, Lord. Please don't let me go through this without learning what You want me to learn. I don't want to be stubborn and hardheaded. God, don't ever take Your velvet hand of discipline from my life. I want to change, to grow. And I know You love me and have my best interests at heart. I trust You."

And with that response, something will begin to take root within us, something wonderful and fulfilling: *the peaceful fruit of righteousness.*

# 74

## A Troubled Soul

*Now My soul has become troubled; and what shall I say, "Father, save Me from this hour"? But for this purpose I came to this hour.*

JOHN 12:27

The hour had come.

The culmination of His purpose here on earth; the culmination of His ministry, of His relationships as He had known them—walking the dusty streets of Galilee, talking around the campfire, eating fish by the seashore; touching, healing, loving. Everything that had been so carefully planned and everything He had accomplished during His earth-walk was coming to an end.

The hour had come. A traumatic hour. An hour of intense suffering and mental anxiety. An hour of separation from His Father. An hour that had been scheduled before the beginning of time. Every minute detail must go as planned.

No small wonder that His soul was troubled!

Does this mean that He had somehow lost the vision that had compelled Him to come to this forlorn place in order that this hour might be fulfilled? No.

Does this mean He was not "acting right" in this very traumatic and intense hour? That His performance was displeasing to God? No.

Does this mean that His faith was weak and wavering? No.

Does this mean that His love and commitment to me—to you—was faltering? No.

Very simply, it means that this God-man was human. It means that He was still very much the Son of Man. A man with emotions reacting to an intensely emotional experience.

Why do we think—where have we learned—that grief or compassion or a "troubled soul" is an indicator of weakness?

He answered His own question with an emphatic "No. This is the hour that I came for. This is the climax of the story. Why, the battle is almost over. I couldn't possibly leave now."

\* \* \*

What "hour" is the reason for my being here? Have I been crying "Save me from this hour" when this could very well be my purpose for coming? And just because my soul is troubled doesn't mean that I'm balking, or reconsidering, or rebelling, or not acting right. It just means I'm human.

Human, yes, but "superhuman" as well, because I have God living within me, who will meet this hour for me. He promised.

> *He gives strength to the weary, And to him who lacks might He increases power.*
>
> ISAIAH 40:29

# 75

## *Used by God in Hard Times*

**We who live are constantly being delivered over to death for Jesus' sake...**

*(Can You tell me why this must be, Lord?)*

**that the life of Jesus also may be manifested in our mortal flesh.**

*(Thank You for Your prompt answer.)*

2 CORINTHIANS 4:11

I wonder.

For those who give God glory and praise and honor in spite of, or in the midst of, their painful, often tragic circumstances, why should God be quick to remove them?

He *knows,* and His compassion for the hurting masses, for the millions who do not know Him, may cause Him to allow my painful circumstances to go unhindered so that others might see His marvelous, sustaining power in my life.

Then again, it may not be the masses or the millions; it may be my son, or my daughter, or my neighbor, or someone that I don't even know. They must see something in *my* life that they need. Am I willing to allow Him to put my life on display? Am I willing to allow Him to make that decision?

*That's a hard question, Lord. Let me think about it.*

Could it be that God has chosen me as one in whose life and circumstances the impossible must be accomplished for Him to be glorified? Could it be He has chosen you?

*I'm willing, Lord.*
*I know You'll be my Strength, regardless.*
*And I trust You. . . .*

# 76

## Sowing in Tears

The pain was *almost* more than he could bear. He had never realized that a broken heart could hurt so terribly, but he couldn't just sit down and cry. It was planting season. So he took his bag of seed and went to the field.

But there was no joy in his work. He didn't hear the clear call of the meadowlark. He didn't see the fields of yellow and lavender on the horizon. The smell of the fresh-turned earth escaped his nostrils. The bite of the pure spring air didn't cause him to lift his head and take in great gulps, for even as he broadcast the tiny seed his eyes were blurred and his hands were damp with tears wiped from his weathered cheeks.

Then, when he could bear it no longer, he fell on his knees and his head touched the broken soil. His tears fell into the furrows, wetting the tiny ovule nestled in the pocket of earth. No one heard. No one saw. There was no one to touch, to care, to say, "I understand."

To know such suffering—*and still to sow.*

\* \* \*

*Those who sow in tears shall reap with joyful shouting. He who goes to and fro weeping, carrying his bag of seed, shall indeed come again with a shout of joy, bringing his sheaves with him.*

PSALM 126:5,6

Yes, you are hurting. But you can't just sit down and cry. The seed would not be planted and growth would never come. There would be no fruit to harvest. No, you must sow. And chances are, there will be no one who really understands . . . no one to touch you or hold you . . . no one to care. To know such suffering—and still to sow.

God's promise is to *you*: Can you believe that one day you will actually SHOUT with sheer joy?

# 77

## *Fixing Our Eyes on Jesus*

*. . . to all who have loved His appearing.*

**2 TIMOTHY 4:8**

*. . . fixing our eyes on Jesus, the author and perfecter of [our] faith.*

**HEBREWS 12:2**

Sunny lifted her head and twisted just slightly until she was staring straight at him. From the very beginning—when she was a tiny little thing—she had learned that he was her source and that she should look to him every minute of the day for growth and strength and beauty. So she did.

Even when it turned dark she knew where he would be when dawn broke, and she would turn to be ready for his appearing. Some days were gloomy and he wouldn't show up, but that was all right. She knew, without an inkling of a doubt, that he was in his place—she just couldn't *see* him. And she knew with that same depth of intensity that he would be there, every day, in the same place. He was the most important thing in her life.

Sunny. A wise little sunflower who, after looking all day at the sun until his face slips below the western horizon, is not deterred by the darkness, but, knowing the promise of his coming, twists and turns expectantly to the east, waiting for his imminent arrival.

*Lord, I need to learn from Sunny, don't I? To know that You are my Source of Life, and that only through You come growth and strength and beauty.*

*I know that. And I know just as surely that You are there—even though it's dark and I may not be able to see you—and that You will always be in "Your place."*

*I say that I "know" it—but is that just information to me?*

*How do I act on what I know?*

*Well, I guess I need to "twist around" and keep looking at You—and I need to anticipate Your return. Oh, not just when everything is ready for the finale and the final curtain call, but that moment when the curtain rises on the day—looking to You, my Source of Life, for You are always there.*

*Lord, remind me to keep looking in the right direction.*

# 78

## *First Encounter*

When I get to Heaven
who will I first meet?
A prophet
very old from ages past?
Or will it be my brother
who died when he was twelve
or Peter, the one they called "The Stone"?

When I get to Heaven
who will I first see?
Joshua
who fought at Jericho?
Or will it be my granddad
my old-time fishin' friend
Or Mary
in her robes of silken gold?

Well, I'm happy
to confess
that all of these
come next to the One
who saved my life

and set me free
for it's
Him
who I'll first meet
yes, it's Him
who I'll first greet
when I die    .
and I go to be with God.

W.M.G.

# 79

## *Blazing a Path*

**Take a new grip with your tired hands,
stand firm on your shaky legs and mark
out a straight, smooth path for your feet
so that those who follow you, though weak
and lame, will not fall and hurt them-
selves, but become strong.**

HEBREWS **12:12,13** TLB

*But, Lord, I'm hurting. I need direction. How in
the world can I possibly mark the path for someone
else when I'm going in circles myself? And it is such
an awesome responsibility to think that someone following me might be weak and lame and depending
on me.*

**Do not fear, for I am with you; Do not anx-
iously look about you, For I am your God.
I will strengthen you, Surely I will help
you, Surely I will uphold you With My
righteous right hand.**

ISAIAH **41:10**

He just reminded me that He is with me. Oh, why do I keep forgetting that? He gives me a firm grip. He enables me to stand with dignity and strength. He's holding my hand. God. Holding *my* hand. Incredible!

If I truly believe this—if I walk in it—then what can come into my life to cause me to flounder? I simply *must* think through these things.

He uses the word "surely," doesn't He? Could He be asking, "Are you telling me that you still don't understand?" When we use "surely," it usually means that we're either exasperated at trying to convince someone of our point or utterly baffled that they didn't realize it in the first place.

All right. I accept this as Truth for me.

Therefore, I *know* that I can stand firm. I can mark a trail. I can be a leader for someone who might be weak and lame . . .

oh, not in *my* strength, but in *His!*

# 80

## *When Jesus Was Gone*

They were huddled together, almost as one, hands locked, arms intertwined, looking dully at the tomb. Their faces were streaked with the tears and dust of the day. THUD! The stone fell and covered the opening, and the sound seemed to draw the last ounce of strength from their weary bodies. They slumped and drew closer. Two Marys: Mary Magdalene and Mary the sister of Lazarus.

What a tragic day it had been! They were awakened with the news that Jesus had been taken captive, and the events that followed had left them numb, ravaged, desolate, *alone.*

Jesus. He had touched their lives. Oh yes, in dramatically different ways, but He was Jesus. They had a common bond. They loved Him. They needed Him. They had believed Him. Now He was gone.

Do you frown on them for their silence? Do you judge them for their tears? Have you never sat and watched a loved one being lowered into a grave? Gone.

I know, good will come. That's a promise. But times such as these are not times to exhort, to teach, to point out how God works through suffering in order to reveal His grand plan. Be quiet and let them grieve. They're lonely. Their hearts have been bruised and broken. They're remembering what their lives were like before Jesus came, trying to imagine life now... *without Him*. They're trying to sort through the confusion; they're frightened by all of the crumbled dreams that will never come to pass; they're wondering why His power was limited... *Couldn't He have done* something? *Oh, Jesus, Jesus. How am I going to face tomorrow without You? You filled my days with purpose and meaning. You made my life so beautiful, and now You're gone! Gone! Oh, no! I love You. I need You. Come back, come back! Please don't leave me.*

* * *

*My precious Lord. I understand their grief. How frightening it would be to think that You would not be in my life tomorrow . . . that You had come—and gone—and all that was left for me was remembering.*

*But no! You are here, beside me . . . inside me. Forever! I will never be without You! You are my Life, my Song, my Hope, my Peace, my Joy, my Strength, my Everything! Thank You that I will never have to experience what dear Mary Magdalene and sweet Mary went through. Would You please tell them that I love them and that I'm looking forward to meeting them?*

# 81

## *Finding Joy and Peace*

My *joy*, my *peace* are no one's responsibility but my own.

I place too great an expectation on any person (including myself) if I hold them responsible for being my *joy* and my *peace*. No. That *joy* and that *peace* are too fragile. They are shallowly rooted in an imperfect source and can blow away with a single breath.

It's my responsibility. And no harsh or unkind word, no rejection, no injustice committed by *anyone* can rob me of my *joy* and my *peace* . . . unless I *let* it.

You see, my *joy* stems from my love relationship with the God-man, Jesus Christ. It's much like a human love relationship. There is joy mingled with the anticipation of being together, talking to each other, sharing, touching, giving. But it isn't fragile like a human love relationship.

My *joy* is, in great part, *security*. Knowing that I am loved and that this Person to whom I have given my love returns that love to me—more so than I can comprehend. Knowing that He will be faithful to me forever and that He will never, never leave me.

My *peace* is basically *trust* in the One who brings me joy.

If I will think on these things instead of on my circumstances or the people around me, instead of majoring on the mistakes and misjudgments of others, instead of focusing on my feelings rather than on His promises to me, then my *joy* and *peace* will remain unscathed. But it is up to me, for only I control my thought processes.

What I put in my mind is like what I put in my mouth. I choose what goes into that "open cave," and when I do, it becomes a part of my system. I have to use sound thinking and strict discipline, or I'll stuff myself, or eat greasy things that upset my stomach, or drink too much caffeine and make my night short, or eat a lot of sweets that cause blemishes on my face.

They say, "You are what you eat." I don't disagree with that. But I don't believe it's the most important fact. "You are what you think." That's most important, for *you will "life-out" whatever you believe about yourself . . .* and believing is a function of your mind.

*Your thoughts make up your world.*
*What do you want your world to be?*

# 82

## *Finding God in the Storm*

**Thou hast been a defense for the helpless, A defense for the needy in his distress, A refuge from the storm, A shade from the heat.**

**ISAIAH 25:4**

Will your imagination work today?
Can you close your eyes and be very still
 for just a few minutes . . .
 placing yourself in the pictures God paints?
He wants to speak to you.

*Lord, I am helpless.
I am in distress, so very
needy;
I am in a raging storm and
the magnitude
of the storm
frightens me.
And oh Lord, I am exhausted because
of the heat*

*the scorching sun*
*the endlessness*
*of a barren*
*forsaken desert.*
*You tell me, Lord,*
*that You are a defense*
*for the helpless*
*and for the needy;*
*that You are a*
*refuge and*
*a shade.*

*Lord, I run to You and*
*cling to you,*
*that You may be ALL of these*
*things in my life.*
*Thank You.*

**He will be as real to you as you allow Him to be.**

# 83

## *His Self-Portrait*

*The Lord says: Let not the wise man bask in his wisdom, nor the mighty man in his might, nor the rich man in his riches. Let them boast in this alone: That they truly know me, and understand that I am the Lord of justice and of righteousness whose love is steadfast, and that I love to be this way.*

JEREMIAH 9:23,24 TLB

JUSTICE: fair
RIGHTEOUSNESS: good
STEADFAST LOVE: loyal, faithful, enduring, firm

God has given me a picture of Himself. These characteristics motivate Him, and they are *always* His underlying purpose.

> I allowed this or I did that because I am always just and righteous and because I love you

*Therefore:*

If what is happening in my life or in the lives of my loved ones does not fit into one of these categories, then I am not viewing it correctly—from the proper perspective. *God does not lie*, and I must keep this in mind constantly.

A. W. Tozer said, "It is most important to our spiritual welfare that we hold in our minds always a right conception of God. *Nothing twists and deforms the soul more than a low or unworthy conception of God.*"*

---

*\*The Best of Tozer* (Grand Rapids, MI: Baker Book House, 1978), p.120.

# 84

## *The Sufferings of This World*

> *You are looking at this only from a human point of view and not from God's.*
>
> **MARK 8:33** TLB

I cringe when I hear someone say, "God took my son," or "God brought this deformed child into my life," or "God caused this tragic accident."

This is looking at things from the human point of view. Nowhere in Scripture does God promise to extract us from the sufferings of this world. And yet so many times it's Him we blame, it's Him we shake our fists at. We live in an alien world, in a fallen world with people who are lost, who have rejected God's love and grace, who are under the control of the Deceiver and his devoted followers. And so we're "fair game." If we're in enemy territory, then we are subject to the enemy's attacks.

Christians must go through the same tragedies, heartaches, and frustrations that non-Christians do. We aren't hiding behind a barricade. We're in an intense battle. Jesus said:

*I have told you these things so that in Me you may have [perfect] peace and confidence. In the world you have tribulation and trials and distress and frustration; but be of good cheer [take courage; be confident, certain, undaunted]! For I have overcome the world. [I have deprived it of power to harm you and have conquered it for you.]*

JOHN 16:33 AMP

He assures us that we will experience difficult times. He also assures us that we will not be destroyed because of these difficult times.

*I have overcome*
*I have robbed it of power to harm*
*I have conquered it.*

He isn't talking about our physical well-being. He is talking about that unshakable identity, that never-failing love, that Spirit that refuses to be bound and defeated. He does not assure us that we will come through unscathed and unscarred, or even alive! The "plus" is that He is our strength. The "plus" is that we are not alone!

Jesus prayed, "I do not ask Thee to take them *out* of the world, but to keep them from the evil one" (John 17:15). God did not keep Jesus from the sufferings of this hostile world, but Jesus held fast to God and Truth. God did not take Him out of the world, but He did keep Him safe from evil. He triumphed over evil. He faced the evil of His day and overcame. He faced each day in the strength of who He was and who God was.

*Because He lives in me, I can do the same.*
*Because He lives in you, you can do the same,*
*can't you?*

# 85

## A Planned Pregnancy

Mary is large with the child in her womb. Her first child . . . and the baby is due just any time now. She watches out the window as Joseph is making preparations for the trip to Bethlehem.

*Oh why must we go to Bethlehem now? I'm so big and uncomfortable. Lord God, I want to be here at home when I have my baby, with my family and friends around to help and encourage me. I don't know anyone at all in Bethlehem. Just to be in my own bedroom. Please, God, let me have my baby here in Nazareth. It's such a little thing to ask of You, and the trip is going to be so long and wearisome and painful for me. Would it matter terribly much where the baby is born?*

Mary might have prayed that way. But then, Mary didn't know that her baby *had* to be born in Bethlehem. You see, the conception took place at the right time for the baby to come when they were in Bethlehem—that was nine months in advance: The shepherds had been chosen; the weather was planned; the star was in the right place; the wise men were on their way; other events in Herod's life had brought his jealousy to the boiling point; every person had carried out his part of the program, even renting all of the available rooms! Everything was ready in Bethlehem for the long-awaited prophecy to be fulfilled. God had made His plans.

Dear, dear Mary. You didn't know all of those things, did you? And it did seem like such a small favor to ask. . . . *O Lord, the prayers I utter are spoken in ignorance of Your plans for my life and Your plans for my beloved family, just like Mary. And sometimes it seems to me that it would be such an easy thing for you to answer my prayer in the way I want You to. To me it isn't an earth-shaking decision, and I've thought it out so carefully.*

*Please, Father, follow through on Your plans. I retract my petition. I didn't realize that You had everything ready.*

❊ ❊ ❊

***This plan of mine is not what you would work out, neither are my thoughts the same as yours! For just as the heavens are higher than the earth, so are my ways higher than yours, and my thoughts than yours.***

ISAIAH 55:8,9 TLB

# 86

## A Father's Words

*My son, give attention to my words;*
*Incline your ear to my sayings. Do not let*
*them depart from your sight; Keep them in*
*the midst of your heart. For they are life to*
*those who find them, And health to all*
*their whole body.*

**PROVERBS 4:20–22**

*MY SON:* This verse is directed to an individual, and since I'm the reader, I can take it as being addressed to me—Anabel. When I'm singled out, addressed in this way so personally, I should be very attentive to what is said.

A father is speaking to a beloved son.

Does he have the authority to speak? Yes.

Will he have his son's best interest at heart? Yes.

Will this advice be based on love? Yes.

*GIVE ATTENTION:* Take notice. Lay aside whatever you are doing. Discipline your eyes, your mind, and your body so that you will have one thing only on which to focus.

*TO MY WORDS:* My rapt attention is to be given to his *words.* I must realize that he is speaking out of the depths of his heart. This is very important to him.

*INCLINE YOUR EAR TO MY SAYINGS:* Cup your hand behind your ear and lean toward the one who's speaking . . . you don't want to miss a single word.

*DO NOT LET THEM DEPART FROM YOUR SIGHT:* "Let" is a word signifying choice. I choose to keep the words before me. Now how I do this will be unique to me, but the command remains. What I see passes through my thinking processes. What I see I think about. It will help me to remember.

*KEEP THEM IN THE MIDST OF YOUR HEART:* Meditate on them. Make room for them in the deepest part of your being. Realize their worth. Plant them so they cannot be lost. Love them. Place them with your most cherished possessions. (My paraphrase: Clutch them closely to your breast.)

*FOR THEY ARE LIFE TO THOSE WHO FIND THEM:* Do I want this "life"? Yes, I do.

A. W. Tozer makes this statement: *"Spiritual gifts and graces come only to those who WANT them badly enough. It may be said without qualification that every man is as holy and as full of the Spirit as he WANTS to* *be. He may not be as full as he WISHES he were, but he is most certainly as full as he WANTS to be."* *

*AND HEALTH TO ALL THEIR WHOLE BODY:* Taylor paraphrases this: "real life and radiant health." God's Word says, "It is appointed for men to die once" (Hebrews 9:27). This is a God-planned process of aging, deterioration, and death. I accept this and do not intend to ask for deliverance from this process. "Radiant health" does not mean that I will never be sick, but radiance emanates from the Spirit in spite of my physical well-being—and I'll settle for that any day.

*Selah*

---

*A.W. Tozer, *The Best of Tozer* (Grand Rapids: Baker Book House, 1978), p.37.

# 87

## A Song in the Night

**God my Maker . . . gives songs in the night.**

JOB 35:10

It is very late.
It is very dark.
It is very quiet.
So quiet that it seems all
the world must be sleeping.

Suddenly a bird begins to sing.
How beautiful!
How clear!
. . . how strange.

*Why is that bird singing, Lord? It is so dark. I doubt that it's because of a full stomach, and the heavy thunderstorm we had this afternoon certainly didn't leave her a dry nest to warble about. Why? Why does she sing?*

*I question whether it could be for her benefit in any way. She doesn't even know anyone is listening.*

She's all by herself in the world out there. I cannot imagine that it is for a sense of "fulfillment" . . . birds don't have that capacity, do they, Lord?

And I am quite sure that it is NOT because she had a "good day." She has worked hard all day getting enough food. Her nest may have been destroyed in the storm; her tiny little ones may have been killed. All sorts of bad things—and yet she sings!

> Is it to make the darkness beautiful?
> Is she serenading her loved one?
> Is it to declare her territorial boundaries?
> Is it a source of comfort from You for those who might be listening?

Lord, regardless of her reason, that little bird is being used by You. She is glorifying You through her song.

I, too, by Your grace, can choose to sing in the night, in the darkness, in the stillness, when I am all alone. Then others will say, "Why is she singing? It's so dark!" And I can answer, "My Maker gives me songs in the night."

**Before He can give me a song,
I must experience the night.**

# 88

## *Resting in God's Promises*

God is our refuge and strength,
A very present help in trouble.
Therefore we will not fear,
Though the earth should change,
And though the mountains slip into
the heart of the sea;
Though its waters roar and foam,
Though the mountains quake at its
swelling pride. Selah.

PSALM 46:1–3

What does this mean to me—today?
How can I grasp it and say "this is mine?"
Step by step—let's claim it together.

God is my place of safety, my fortress, my hiding place, my shelter. Therefore, *I am safe.*

**I accept this Truth as mine.**

He is the Source of my power, my Enabler, my ability to perform and my abililty to persevere. He is my tenacity, my strength. My very *Life.* I am *not* to meet any crisis in my own strength.

**I accept this Truth as mine.**

He is a very *present* help. He is here. And He isn't so involved with gigantic world problems that He doesn't have time for mine. He is *interested.* He is never away from me, especially when I am in need, hurting, weary, perplexed, or in a troublesome setting of *any* kind. I am *never* by myself. He is always with me and He understands.

**I accept this Truth as mine.**

Now, because I have *accepted* this as Truth, because I believe this, I will not fear. Fear only for myself? No, I will not fear for those who are dear to me, either. So I will not allow anything that might result in my experiencing apprehension, anxiety, or confusion to cause me alarm—*because I can depend on Him.*

**I accept this Truth as mine.**

Even if the earth around me (my environment) should be thrown into a state of upheaval, and even if the very mountains quake (those things I presumed to be unshakable), and even if the sea around me (the world and its multitudes) should become hostile and fierce and cause violent unrest, *I will not fear.*

I WILL NOT FEAR. This *does not mean* that my emotions won't go haywire, that my knees will never get weak, that my heart will never beat like a trip-hammer, or that my hands will never tremble. I cannot control my emotions or the effect they have on my body. I *control* my thoughts and rest in His promises.

**I accept this Truth as mine.**

*When my anxious thoughts multiply*
    *within me,*
*Thy consolations delight my soul.*

PSALM 94:19

# 89

## *Safe at Last*

Ready to fly away with me?
Our borders are limitless! Our confinement
is as narrow as we allow it to be.

*Oh, that I had the wings of a dove!*
*I would fly away and be at rest—*
*I would flee far away and stay in the desert;*
*I would hurry to my place of shelter,*
*far from the tempest and storm.*

PSALM 55:6–8 NIV

The dove
     has neither claw nor sting
     nor weapon
     for the fight.
She owes her safety to the wing
     her victory to flight!
The Bridegroom
     opens His arms of love
     and in them folds
     the panting dove.*

---

*H. W. Smith

It is in my mind, on His wings of Truth, that I flee to my place of safety—my shelter—the arms of my Bridegroom. Sometimes I am so out of breath when I get there—all "trembly" and panting, dove-like. But He holds me tenderly and speaks gently—assuring me of His love and His protection. And I rest. Safe.

# 90

## *God's Plan or Mine?*

*I have given my loved one to You, Lord. Please send what he needs: storm or sunshine, turbulence or calm, rain or snow, fruit or barrenness. You have made him and You know. I trust You.*

Do I really?
God usually gives me
a chance to find out if I trust Him or not. . . .

* * *

I was praying for Pres' back and had "told" God exactly what I wanted and how I believed the events should come about—NOW!

*Lord, Pres has been victorious in this over the years, and he is hurting so badly. I really don't see that having this pain linger any longer can profit anyone. So I humbly ask you to heal his back . . . today.* (An abbreviated version.)

**God:**
These are the plans that you have for Pres, Anabel?

**Anabel:**
*Yes, Lord.*

**God:**
These are the plans you would like for Me to carry out?

**Anabel:**
*Yes, Lord.*

**God:**
I, too, have some plans for Pres. Would you like for Me to abandon MY plans and go with yours?

**Anabel:**
(Silence. Now, what was that statement I was wondering about—if I really believed it? You remember, don't you? That one about giving my loved one to Him and trusting Him.)

A very quiet answer: *No, Lord. I want You to do it Your way, please. I do trust You, my dear Jesus . . . implicitly.*

# 91

## The Lamp and the Power

*We have this treasure in earthen vessels,*
*that the surpassing greatness of the power*
*may be of God and not from ourselves.*

2 CORINTHIANS 4:7

The "treasure" Paul is talking about is the gospel. I recognize that; but all the same, it's difficult for me to think of myself as an "earthen vessel" or a "perishable container" (the translation in *The Living Bible*).

When I think of perishable containers, I think of paper cups and tin cans and broken vases. They don't have any life! They can't think and choose and cry and get mad like I do. And I certainly don't see myself as God's hand puppet or marionette, there for all His string-pulling needs.

*What do You mean, Lord? I don't understand.*

Paul makes a distinction between *me* and my *earthen vessel:* " . . . *We* have this treasure in earthen vessels. . . ." So I'm in there with the treasure in my possession: the Person of the gospel, Jesus Christ. It's more like

Aladdin and the magic lamp. I have this wonderful Presence within me.

But wait. Aladdin's lamp just sat around gathering dust until he discovered how to release the power inside. *Is that the key, Lord? Releasing the power inside? Am I a useless lamp that gathers dust until the power is released?* Come to think of it, that would be a more exact analogy because I can do a lot of things without His power. Destructive, hurtful, unkind, thoughtless, careless things that His power would not do.

The comparison is applicable: Only when I "release" His power do I see how futile *my* attempts at power-playing have been. In my earthen vessel I can either gather dust or stir it up through all the wonderful and magnificent acts that I perform by His power through me. I can gather dust or I can create a whirlwind. And the choice is mine. Gathering dust is the limit of *my* ability. But the God inside me makes whirlwinds.

God did not create us to trust and believe in *ourselves,* in our *own* adequacy. No. He longs to strip us bare and take us to the place where we must depend on Him, on His spirit within us. Then, by His grace, He takes us by the hand and teaches us that we can trust and rest *completely* in Him, in *His* strength and power.

*We must learn the lesson of dependence before we can move on to the lesson of confidence.*

Confidence? Yes. Only after we learn that we can do nothing without Him do we learn that when we release

Him, our "perishable containers" are capable of accomplishing mighty things. And therein lies our confidence: in Him.

*I can do all things through Him who strengthens me. . . .*

*Not that we are adequate in ourselves to consider anything as coming from ourselves, but our adequacy is from God. . . .*

*Apart from Me you can do nothing.*

PHILIPPIANS 4:13
2 CORINTHIANS 3:5
JOHN 15:5

*Lord,*

*My perishable container isn't quite what it used to be (remember that song about "the old gray mare"?). How I praise You that the Power within me is ageless. That my ability to perform is not the key to success. My ability to allow You to perform is the key to success. Of course, I may not climb high mountains or run races like I used to do, but there are different mountains to climb and different races to be run.*

*I am so glad that I'm the lamp and You're the Power.*

# 92

## The One to Turn To

I don't know where you are this morning in your emotions
and your thoughts, but perhaps this will help you
verbalize your feelings to Him:

> *Hear my cry, O God;*
> *Give heed to my prayer.*
> *From the end of the earth I call to Thee*
> *When my heart is faint;*
> *Lead me to the rock that is higher than I.*
> *For Thou hast been a refuge for me,*
> *A tower of strength against the enemy.*
> *Let me dwell in Thy tent forever;*
> *Let me take refuge in the*
> *shelter of Thy wings.*

**PSALM 61:1–4**

*　*　*

*O God, please hear me when I cry out to You,*
*please listen as I pour out my heart.*
*It doesn't matter where I am—*
*how far away from home I might be.*

*You are the One I turn to*
*when things just seem to*
*be too much for me—*
*when I'm fighting anxiety*
*or depression, fear or anything*
*that causes me to become*
*discouraged.*
*O Lord, cause me to look to You,*
*for You are so strong,*
*so stable, so powerful and wise.*
*You have always been the*
*One to whom I turn for*
*solace, for strength,*
*for understanding—You have*
*always been the Source of*
*my strength against*
*the satanic forces in*
*this world.*

*Thank You, dear Father, that*
*I am seated with You—*
*secure in You*
*strong in You*
*sheltered in Your arms and*
*hidden beneath Your wings.*

# 93

*If . . .*

**If Christ has not been raised, then our preaching is vain and your faith also is vain.**

1 CORINTHIANS **15:14**

If . . . locked in my chamber of unchallenged fears
   I wait for the dawn
   with curtains drawn

If . . . alone in that darkness I cry to be free
   yet claim that my Captor
   has swallowed the key

If . . . I cling to my memories living only the past
   and doubting the future
   I give up at last

If . . . in the midst of this battle I turn and retreat
   blind to my victory and
   accepting defeat

Then Christ has died needlessly
And peace is a fantasy
Then hope is a wounded word
"The coming King" is but a phrase I've heard . . .
    and all the world is lost.

W.M.G.

*Lord, I believe.*
*Help me in my unbelief.*

# 94

## The Test Drive

You talk about flashy!

Nat had seen this car in his fantasy since he was five years old.

The vivid colors were exactly as he had planned: deep blue-green, royal purple, and, even though no one else had especially liked it, a hair-thin line of lime green stretching from front to back, where there were gold numbers and a gold emblem. There wasn't a lot of chrome, but it was there in just the right proportion. And the lines were such that this car and the wind would be one—no resistance at all. Beautiful! That was all you could say about it. Beautiful.

And no expense had been spared. It was as finely tuned inside as it was finely designed outside. He had spent hours upon hours on the car, and the hours had blended into months and years—drawing and dreaming, working and planning, building and tearing down and rebuilding again. And now it was finished. It was ready.

*But was it really?*

There's only one way to determine how *ready* it really is: Drive it. Put it through strenuous testing. Let it meet the adversities of the racetrack. Right?

* * *

*I know, my God, that you test men to see if they are good; for you enjoy good men.*

1 CHRONICLES 29:17 TLB

The outside is just for show, isn't it?
God knows what's "under the hood" —what's inside of me.
I must be tested for performance.
Not for His satisfaction. For mine.
And the finish won't surprise Him.

# 95

## The Strength to Go On

*From Bucharest, Romania*
*Holy Week, 1977*

The circumstances in which you find yourself may be very, very difficult. You want to understand, but it is beyond your ability just now. Perhaps this testimony will encourage you to stand—to trust—to rest.

*On Wednesday, Pavel Nicolescu was severely beaten, worse than any of the others. The bruises were still evident as we gathered together on Good Friday, and he was still trembling with pain. When it came his time to speak, he said:*

*"Brothers, you know I cannot pray, 'Lord get me out of this trouble or out of this place,' because I believe He wills that I be here. And if I pray, 'Lord, get me out of here,' I am actually saying, 'God, take me out of Your will.' So the only thing I can pray is, 'Lord, give me strength and courage to go on and do here what You expect me to do.'"*

*And now, Lord, take note of their threats, and grant that Thy bondservants may speak Thy word with all confidence.*

Acts 4:29

*Lord, I* must have *Your strength and Your courage to go on and do what You expect me to do. I simply cannot do it! I'm hurting too badly. Oh, may I have the boldness to proclaim Your sufficiency, Your presence, Your love to those around me who are watching me, controlling me, judging me as I endure this pain. Thank You, sweet Jesus, for Your strength.*

---

# 96

## *Choosing Freedom*

Your life is a mess?
Your days are filled with hassles and pressures?
There are times when the pain is so intense
　　physically or emotionally
　　that you want to fall into a limp heap on the floor
　　and yell "uncle"
　　or disappear into the darkness of the closet
　　and close the door?
The circumstances cannot be changed.
You're in them and there's no way out.
The door is locked.

Let me give you a word of encouragement.

❊ ❊ ❊

What do we mean when we speak of the "soul"?
Well, the word "soul" comes from the Greek word
*psyche,* referring to the invisible part of you, your personality (your mind, your will, and your emotions). Your
soul is the real you—the person who laughs and talks,
yells at the ball game, cries at sad movies, and sorts out
all the information that comes into your mind.

There are people who are *physically* handicapped, whose bodies don't function as they should, but their soul functions. It's like they're in solitary confinement. There isn't any vehicle through which they can talk to the outside world. Their defective body has imprisoned their soul because of its inability to receive messages *from* the soul or give messages *to* the soul. But the soul is all right—the "real" person.

Keeping that illustration of the soul in mind and realizing that the soul can be "separated," so to speak, from the body, consider this verse:

> *Our soul has escaped as a bird out of the snare of the trapper; The snare is broken and we have escaped.*
>
> PSALM 124:7

Do you see that though you may be mired in difficult or even tragic circumstances, your soul is capable of escape?

Do you see that your ability to think and to choose, regardless of your circumstances, is free?

Oh, you can't *choose* to walk away from those circumstances, but you *can choose* to not let them control your thoughts.

Your soul is free to wander where it will. The physical limitations that have been imposed on you in this world cannot place limitations on your soul.

You *choose* with your free will what you are going to set your mind on.

Of course, your emotions won't understand—they don't have the capacity to understand, remember? They just feel.

> But *you* have been set free!
> *For prison bars*
> *cannot control*
> *the flight*
> *the freedom*
> *of my soul.*

# 97

## Are You Settled in Your Mind?

**He is settled in his mind that Jehovah will take care of him.**

PSALM 112:7 TLB

She was going through a sordid divorce. Her life, her reputation, her mothering, her personality—*everything* was being cut open and dissected and shredded. The financial security to which she had become accustomed was gone; the post office had been notified that her prestigious address had changed. And Tuesday, another chapter would be added to her manila file in court: *Jan vs. Tom.*

I saw her on Wednesday and was expecting to find her slumped in her chair, head down, eyes red-rimmed—defeated.

"Jan! How did it go yesterday? Did you make it all right?"

"All right? Hey! I'm on top of it! Let me show you something."

And she began digging in her skirt pocket for what turned out to be a crumpled scrap of paper.

"Look at this, Anabel."

I took it and smoothed it out. It was written in pencil, so it was smeared and not all that legible, but there it was:

*Jan, Jehovah will take care of you . . .*

and He did.

Jan was settled in her mind.

＊ ＊ ＊

If I truly believe that God is at work in my life, purifying, shaping, conforming me to the beauty of His image . . .

If I truly believe He allows certain things to come into my life for the completion of His purpose . . .

If I truly believe that He is a loving God and has no intention of hurting me, having only my best interests at heart . . .

Then how should I view each day?

How should I accept each stressful event?

How should I accordingly behave?

My habit is to excuse my misbehavior with pet, pat phrases:

> "I'm awfully tired . . . "
> "It was all his fault . . . "
> "After all these years, I'm just going to quit trying . . . "
> "It might work for others, but not for me . . . "
> "I just can't do it . . . "

"God's expectations of me are way out
of line . . . "
"It's that time of month . . . "

These excuses are antiquated, worn-out, stifling, and, simply put, *just not true.*

There is one—and only one—question to ask myself:

<u>Do</u> *I truly believe?*
*Do <u>I</u> truly believe?*
*Do I <u>truly</u> believe?*
*Do I truly <u>believe</u>?*

To answer "yes" will settle my mind on any issue.

# 98

# Easter Thoughts for Every Day

He is risen! Risen . . . *indeed?*
And what is that to mean to me?

> I live each day as best I can;
> I reach out to my fellowman.
> I sometimes slip
> I sometimes sin
> But I always get up and try again!
>
> I read my Bible;
> I know how to pray.
> I try to walk the Christian way.
> I know God cares
> And I believe He sees
> That the only desire of my heart is to please.

He is risen! Risen . . . *indeed?*
And what is that to mean to me?

> *It is very plain it means nothing to you*
> *For I see your hand in all you do.*
> *He could still be dead and bound in the grave*

*And He would not have lost His power to save.*
*But don't you see? Can't you comprehend?*
*The tomb was the beginning—not the end.*
*His death was not all He had to give—*
*He arose that we might have the power to live!*

He is risen! Risen . . . *indeed?*
And what is that to mean to me?

    You mean that both of us died that day
    In some mysterious "God-planned" way?
    That *my* hands are useless
    *My* lips are dumb
    *My* eyes are sightless
    *My* heart is numb?
    *Yet the power to live is mine at last?*
    The days of striving and failing are past?
    Praise God! At last the truth I see—
    He is risen!
    He lives!
    *He lives through me!*

# 99

## *Praying for Victory*

**M**y son Pres was going through a humiliating experience brought about by spineless men who pre-
tended to exemplify the Christian life. They sang in the
choir and took up the offering and served as deacons.
Preposterous! It was so unfair, so wrong! And we were
helpless to come against their proud, worldly authority.

> I prayed: *Lord, if You can alter Your plans for this
> loved one without hindering Your sover-
> eign purpose for his life, I humbly ask You
> to do so.*

He didn't alter the plans. The circumstances were
not changed. You see, God's plans for Pres were far
deeper than mine. He was building Christlike character.
My plan was to protect my son from disappointment and
pain and preserve his world-system image.

I am slowly coming to see the *audacity* of my ap-
proaching the Lord and even *suggesting* my plan. If you
study the prayers of Paul you'll find that *he did not pray
that the circumstances of His people might be changed,
but that they might be victorious* in the circumstances.

* * *

*It was a turn of events from the Lord that He might establish His word. . . .*

1 KINGS 12:15

*"This thing has come from Me." So they listened to the word of the Lord, and returned and went their way . . .*

1 KINGS 12:24

*The hand of the Lord has done this, and the Holy One of Israel has created it . . . that they may see and recognize and consider and gain insight . . .*

ISAIAH 41:20

*I am God and there is no other; I am God and there is no one like Me, declaring the end from the beginning and from ancient times things which have not been done, saying, "My purpose will be established, and I will accomplish all My good pleasure."*

ISAIAH 46:9,10

*Lord, I do not know what to ask.*
*Thank You that You know what to give.*

# 100

## *The Gift Too Wonderful for Words*

**Thanks be to God for His Gift,
[precious] beyond telling
[His indescribable, inexpressible, free Gift]!**

**II Corinthians 9:15 AMP**

*Precious Heavenly Father,*

*I want to say to You, "Thank You."*

*Oh, I thank You for so many beautiful things
that have come from Your hand alone—innumerable
gifts. (Maybe I didn't see the "beauty" at first of some
of Your gifts, but I did later on.)*

*But it all began with the one—the best You had
to give. It would have been so easy to give from Your
vast wealth, for "the world is Mine, and all it con-
tains" (Psalm 50:12).*

*But no, You chose to give Your Son. Your only
Son. This was Your first Gift. God forbid that I
should be careless, that I should treat shabbily, mis-
use, or be ungrateful for this incredible Gift to me.*

*That one Gift changed my life. It has made all the difference.*

*So I thank You, dear God, for Jesus, Your inexpressible, indescribable Gift—too wonderful for words.*

# 101

## Cleanse Me, Lord

I would have changed my route just to avoid the unpleasant smell, but I wasn't familiar with the area so I had to stay on the path. Eventually I came to the source of the odor—a stagnant, swampy pool of water apparently left standing after a heavy rain.

I stood looking at that miserable blight in the beauty of the woods: murky, tepid water with slimy-looking weeds and rotted debris under the surface; insects hovering over the dingy quagmire; parched and peeling earth where there used to be some sort of moisture, and then a rank slough bordering the putrid water; and all the while the stench, foul and heavy.

Then the thought surfaced . . .

> *. . . men who are stagnant in spirit . . .*
>
> **ZEPHANIAH 1:12**

STAGNANT:
>       not moving or flowing
>       foul from standing still
>       sluggish, dull

Lord, how tragic!

To be so offensive and unlovely and treacherous. Stagnant.

To be dull and filled with trash. Stagnant. When I could be clear and filled with Your presence.

To be so foul that people would actually take a different path rather than rub shoulders with me. Stagnant.

To actually be such a blight that someone might lose their sense of direction and become lost because of seeing and smelling and touching me! Stagnant.

Lord, please don't ever let me be that way. I know there might have to be some radical cleansing involved to purify my pond, perhaps painful and deep. But rather suffer than be stagnant . . .

repulsive, filthy, sickening, putrid, dead.

Stagnant in my spirit.

# 102

## *Grace in Times of Need*

Let me ask you a question: When does God give us "grace"? Oh, I know, every act of God is full of grace. But specifically . . .

> *Let us therefore draw near with confidence to the throne of grace, that we may receive mercy and may find grace to help in time of need.*
>
> **HEBREWS 4:16**

Answer: "in time of need." In trials, tribulation, distress, wilderness experiences, illness, suffering . . . whatever defines your unique "time of need."

Now, ponder this:

> *Be careful that none of you fails to respond to the grace of God, for if he does there can spring up in him a bitter spirit which can poison the lives of many others.*
>
> **HEBREWS 12:15** PHILLIPS

*  *  *

*Lord, I'm hurting. I am in a time of need. I want people to encourage me, to understand, to hurt with me. But I certainly don't want to <u>use</u> this time of pain to play on the emotions of others, seeking to get my needs met by clinging to the burden instead of responding to Your grace. I agree. There is extreme danger in becoming bitter when people do not meet my expectations, or becoming bitter when the pain doesn't seem to subside. Help me to be discerning, Lord. The desire of my heart is to walk in the provision that You have given me . . .*

*Your amazing, immeasurable grace.*

# 103

## *Thorns*

*I fall upon the thorns of life, I bleed!*
P.B. Shelley

THORNS DO NOT PRICK
*UNLESS*
YOU FALL AGAINST THEM.

So there are "thorns" in your life—
don't pretend they aren't there.

That would deny God the chance
to wrap the thorns with roses
and would prevent the fragrance
of your testimony from
delighting and encouraging others.

No. Don't do that.

Just don't *lean* on them
or
work with them till your
fingers are bloody

or
*grab* them and strap them
to your back
or
cradle them
in your arms . . .

STAND BACK . . .
And watch how God handles thorns!

*The Lord will fight for you while you keep silent.*

EXODUS 14:14

*Do not fear or be dismayed because of this great multitude, for the battle is not yours but God's.*

2 CHRONICLES 20:15

*In all these things we overwhelmingly conquer through Him who loved us.*

ROMANS 8:37

*Stand [we] will, for the Lord is able to make[us] stand.*

ROMANS 14:4

# 104

## *No More Time to Pray*

Seeking answers—needing answers—crying for answers—when action *now* is essential, unavoidable. There's no more time for prayer.

*What do I do, Lord?*

We must study all the teachings and examples of the Lord. In the Garden of Gethsemane Jesus was facing the most difficult experience of His walk on planet Earth. He prayed passionately, entreating the heavenly Father three times to change the circumstances that were before Him. Not six. Not twelve. *THREE* (Matthew 26:36–46).

> He had no more time to pray.
> The circumstance was upon Him.
> He believed He had God's answer, so
> He arose and pursued the course of action
> open to Him.

When you are faced with your own "most difficult" experience, you may pray passionately, entreating God to change the circumstances that are before you. But when there is no more time for prayer and action is absolutely essential, you must arise and pursue the course of action open to you.

Remember, Jesus knew the plan (Luke 18:31–33) but still pleaded with God about it in the Garden. And why not? He was facing intense suffering, rejection, pain, humiliating abuse, and death. He received "no" for His answer, but also received *grace* to meet the coming conflict. So when it came time for action, He was ready: "Arise, let us be going; behold, the one who betrays Me is at hand!"

Remember . . .

*We too receive GRACE when God says "no."*

# 105

## Like a Child at Rest

*To rest.*
What a pleasant thought.

**Surely I have composed and quieted my soul; Like a weaned child rests against his mother, My soul is like a weaned child within me.**

PSALM **131:2**

**I am quiet now before the Lord, just as a child who is weaned from the breast. Yes, my begging has been stilled.**

PSALM **131:2** TLB

Where once, when close to his mother he kept searching and wanting, restless, feeling that in this position he should be receiving—having his needs met, being fulfilled, constantly pampered—now he is content to be held, content with her closeness. He makes no demands. He is quiet. He is still.

## NO ONE ENJOYS
## HOLDING A HYPERACTIVE CHILD.

✿ ✿ ✿

*Lord, I long to be quiet, to rest in Your arms, to desire nothing, to be content just to be in Your presence. The things that I think I need, the obstacles that I think need to be moved, the changes that I believe need to take place in my life—are they really that urgent? You have not abdicated Your throne. You are still very much in control of my affairs and You love me and want what's best for me.*

*To accept this truth and cease to beg, cease to whimper and cry as a pampered child denied at feeding time . . . I want this in my life, O precious Lord.*

*Hold me, please.*

# 106

## *My Stability*

*Sarah, too, had faith, and because of this she was able to become a mother in spite of her old age, for she realized that God, who gave her his promise, would certainly do what he said.*

**HEBREWS 11:11** TLB

According to this verse, Sarah was able to conceive because of her faith. She was able to do this (have a child when it was naturally impossible) because she believed that *the One who had given the promise was* <u>utterly trustworthy</u>.

This must be my position. My stability. He has given *me* a promise, too:

*I am confident of this very thing, that He who began a good work in you <u>will perfect it</u> until the day of Christ Jesus.*

**PHILIPPIANS 1:6**

Do I really believe that He will *certainly do what He said?*

Do I really believe that He is *utterly trustworthy?*

\* \* \*

*Lord, I want to believe, and oh! I need to believe! It just seems that You move so slowly. Not in my life especially, but in the lives of my children. You promise that You are working to perfect them, precious Lord. I can't do anything else. They're away from home and all grown up. I can't tell them what to do, and even to make suggestions seems to irritate them at times. Only You can cover my mistakes and right their wrongs. Only You can draw them to Yourself. I believe that. I rest in that. And I know that You will do what You have promised.*

# 107

## *God's Plan for My Pain*

I really resist (or do I resent?) the trite words that are often given as sage advice to someone who is going through difficult times.

*Well, just think about poor Aunt Pearl (or your sister, or someone you knew thirteen years ago, or someone you don't even know). What if you were in her shoes? You can always find someone who has more problems than you do. Be thankful that yours are not as bad as theirs. Just think about that . . . you know, walking in their moccasins for two weeks.*

Nope. That's not what I need to hear. I don't want my needs or my circumstances to be minimized. They are very real to me. Pressing. Hurting. Stressful. No two problems are alike. Your needs are critically important to you. My needs are critically important to me.

God doesn't minimize my needs or compare them with "Aunt Pearl's," but comparing God's *grace* with my needs blows the cobwebs out of my thinking wheels. How *big* is God's grace? Big enough to take care of my needs? Oh, yes.

But the difficulty arises both in *allowing* Him to meet my needs—in His way, in His timing—and in determining what my *real* need *is*. I may think it's money to pay a debt when He would say, "No, Anabel. You need to learn discipline in taking care of the material things I have given you." I may think my need is release from a circumstance that I am in when He would tenderly admonish me, "No, my sweet Anabel. You need to practice endurance." I may be praying for release from pain. *This, Lord, is my need*. Once again He would say, "No, Anabel. You need to learn true compassion."

*So once again I say, "I trust You, Lord." You have made me and You are now busy conforming me to Your image. I want that. I don't want the pain and the stress and the frustration, but I can't have one without the other. I guess it's kind of like having a baby. It would be nice to have him without the nine months of being nauseated and the discomfort of carrying him around all the time in my tummy, not to mention the intense pain of helping him make his way into our world. But that's a part of motherhood. I can't separate one from the other.*

*My deepest thanks to You, my precious Lord, for your willingness to go through all of these things with me . . . for me . . . through me . . . and for letting me know the expected outcome: to be like You.*

*We know that God causes all things to work together for good to those who love God, to those who are called according to His purpose. For whom He foreknew He also predestined to become conformed to the image of His Son, that He might be the firstborn among many brethren.*

ROMANS 8:28,29

# 108

## *Jesus' Transforming Touch*

"Hey, Shorty! What's your rush?"

*Shorty! I <u>hate</u> that name! If I weren't in such a hurry I'd collar that smartmouth and raise his taxes a few hundred denarii!*

They used to call him Shorty when he was a kid, but few dared to now. He was the chief tax collector, he was wealthy, and he could make life very miserable for anyone who upset his giant ego.

The winding streets of Jericho were almost impassable. Donkeys. Carts. People. People *everywhere.*

*I hope I don't see anyone I know. Here I am, acting just as crazy as everybody else. Pushing and shoving. And for what? To see a self-proclaimed prophet! But I've got to see Him. <u>I've just got to see Him</u>! Story after story of how He's changed people . . . and God knows I need a change! I'm probably the most hated man in town. My cronies hang around like vultures. Huh. I could safely say that I don't have a friend—a single friend. I wonder about my wife's love at times . . . really messed up.*

*But why <u>would</u> anyone love me? Eh, I've made my own bed—I know that. But I'm sick of sneers and* *catcalls wherever I go. I'm sick of living in a virtual palace surrounded by people who hate my guts . . . wondering which servants are loyal . . . having to have someone taste my soup and my wine just in case. . . I hate what I have become. I have what I've always wanted, and I'm sick of all of it! I'd change places with my gardener if I could. I am a wretched, unhappy man! Get out of my way, you peons! Don't you know who you're shoving around? Drat this new robe. It's tripping me.*

*There He is. Over there surrounded by that simpering mass of sick people. But I can't see Him! Wait, I'll climb this sycamore tree. Who would ever believe that the leading tax collector of Jericho was climbing a stupid tree to see what was going on? I've slipped a notch or two.*

*There. There He is. And He's walking this way! Is He looking at me? I'm up here—in the sycamore tree. Hey! Look this way. . . .*

"Hello, Zaccheus! You have a ringside seat, don't you My friend? Well, hurry and come down. I must stay at your house today."

Try to imagine the surprise, the warmth of wonder that came over Zaccheus. . . .

He smiled at Jesus and then ripped a big hole in his fancy new garment as he half climbed and half fell down from his high position.

The crowds parted to let them walk through, but he could hear them grumbling about Jesus going to his house for a meal. He heard the names they were calling him. And he knew Jesus heard them, too.

They walked in silence for a while, and then Zaccheus said, "Lord, I've mistreated a lot of people in my life, and I really can't blame them for the things they say. But, Lord, I'll give half of my possessions to the poor, and if I have defrauded anyone, I'll give him back four times as much! I will."

"Why, I know you will. I've been watching you—looking forward to our meeting today. And I saw you climbing up in the sycamore tree. Pretty good stunt for a man your size and age. Today, Zaccheus, salvation has come to your house."

"I just had to see You, Lord. Somehow or another I knew this was it for me. I couldn't have gone on. But You knew that too, of course.

"By the way, Lord, my friends call me Shorty."*

* * *

Zaccheus left two "high positions" that day.

His new performance was in keeping with who he became after the Lord touched his life. I would like to have been with him as he became a different man, watching the incredulous looks that would follow him as he went from house to house, giving instead of taking. I'm confident that he found great joy in his work. He probably sold his big, fine house, started spending time

---

*See* Luke 19:1–10.

with his wife and his children, started having the most unsuspected, unpretentious guests over for supper.

Oh, I know. I'm putting words in his mouth. I'm adding details that aren't there. I'm drawing a picture of a man I've never seen and I'm speculating on the changes that took place in his life. But the point is this: *Jesus causes people to change.*

*Don't be afraid to climb up into the tree.*

# Other Good
# Harvest House Reading

### THE CONFIDENT WOMAN
by *Anabel Gillham*

The author spent her life trying to be the perfect wife, mother, and Christian. But her life was light-years away from her dream. A passionate look at the transforming power of surrender to God.

### LIFETIME GUARANTEE
by *Bill Gillham*

You've tried fixing your marriage, your kids, your job. Suddenly the light dawns. It's not your problems that need fixing, it's your life! The good news is that the Christian is backed by a lifetime guarantee.

### HE SAID, SHE SAID
by *Bill and Anabel Gillham*

On the outside the Gillhams were trying hard to do everything right for a happy marriage, but on the inside they were deeply hurting. Candid conversations about how Christ in you can transform your entire marriage.

### GOD WHISPERS IN THE NIGHT
by *Marie Shropshire*

As we journey through life, we can become ensnared by trials, hurt, and grief. These gentle words of comfort are an invitation to rest in God's arms and let His healing touch renew our peace and hope.

### LOVING GOD WITH ALL YOUR MIND
by *Elizabeth George*

Making every thought pleasing to God can be a challenge when you're drained by fear, worry, or sadness. Elizabeth shows women how to enjoy a more vibrant love relationship with God.